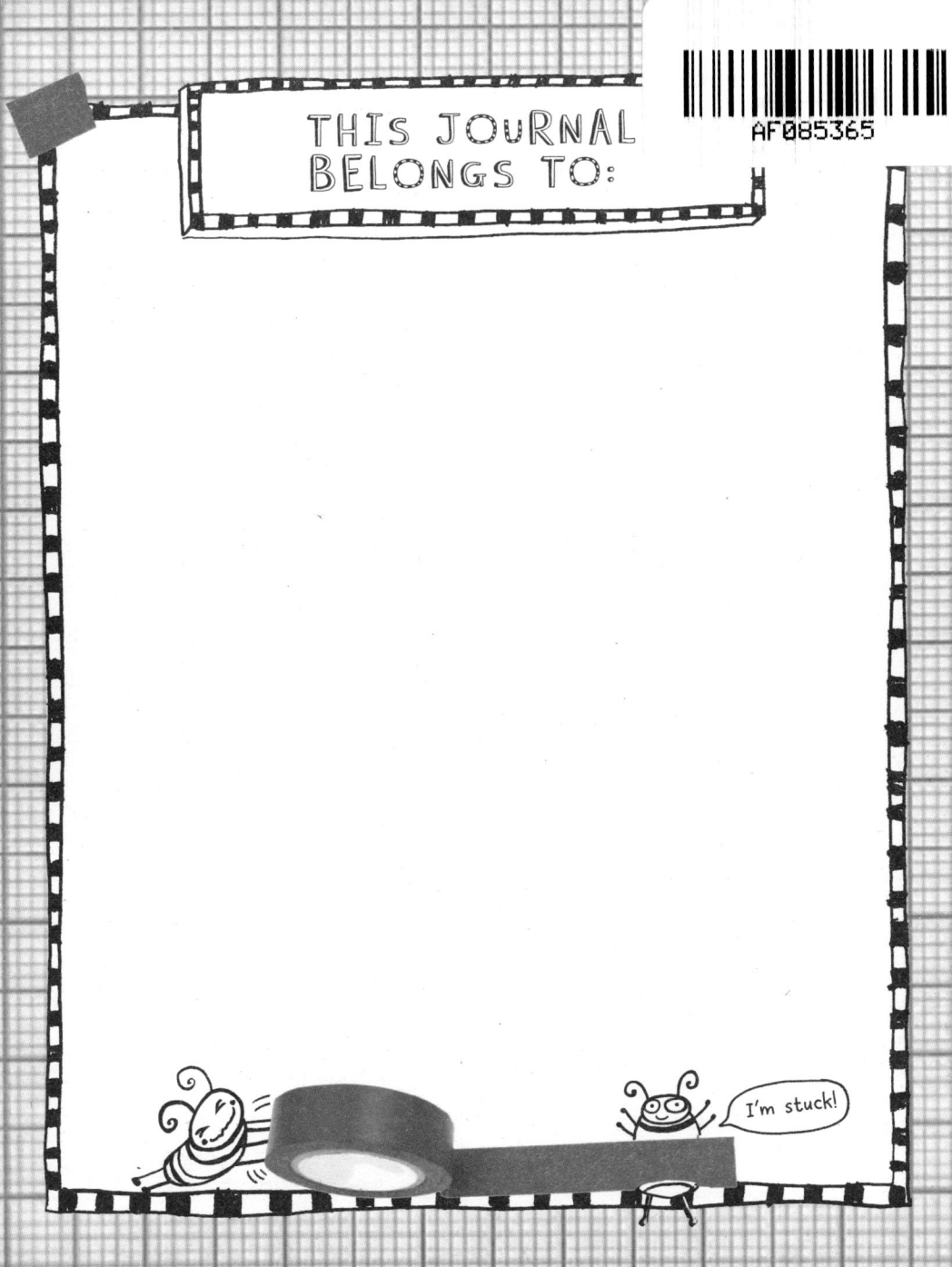

This book is dedicated to:

Toby and his mum, Zoe ♥

Isaac and his Aunty Wendy ♥

Zoë and her Aunty Lauren ♥

Hope you enjoy making this book your own!
♥

A very special THANK YOU to the wonderful Sheila Vaughan. Much love from me, Liz xx

Thank you to Team Scholastic, Lyn and Jason too
♥

HOW TO USE THIS JOURNAL

FILL up *EVERY* page with COLOUR! Use your imagination to draw pictures and write down interesting things. Write about what you ☺ like and don't like. ☹ Collect stuff to stick in the pages. This journal is YOURS ♡ and you should have FUN on every page. So when you are old (like the Fossils), you can look back at your journal and say, "Wow! This is the work of a GENIUS."

(True.)

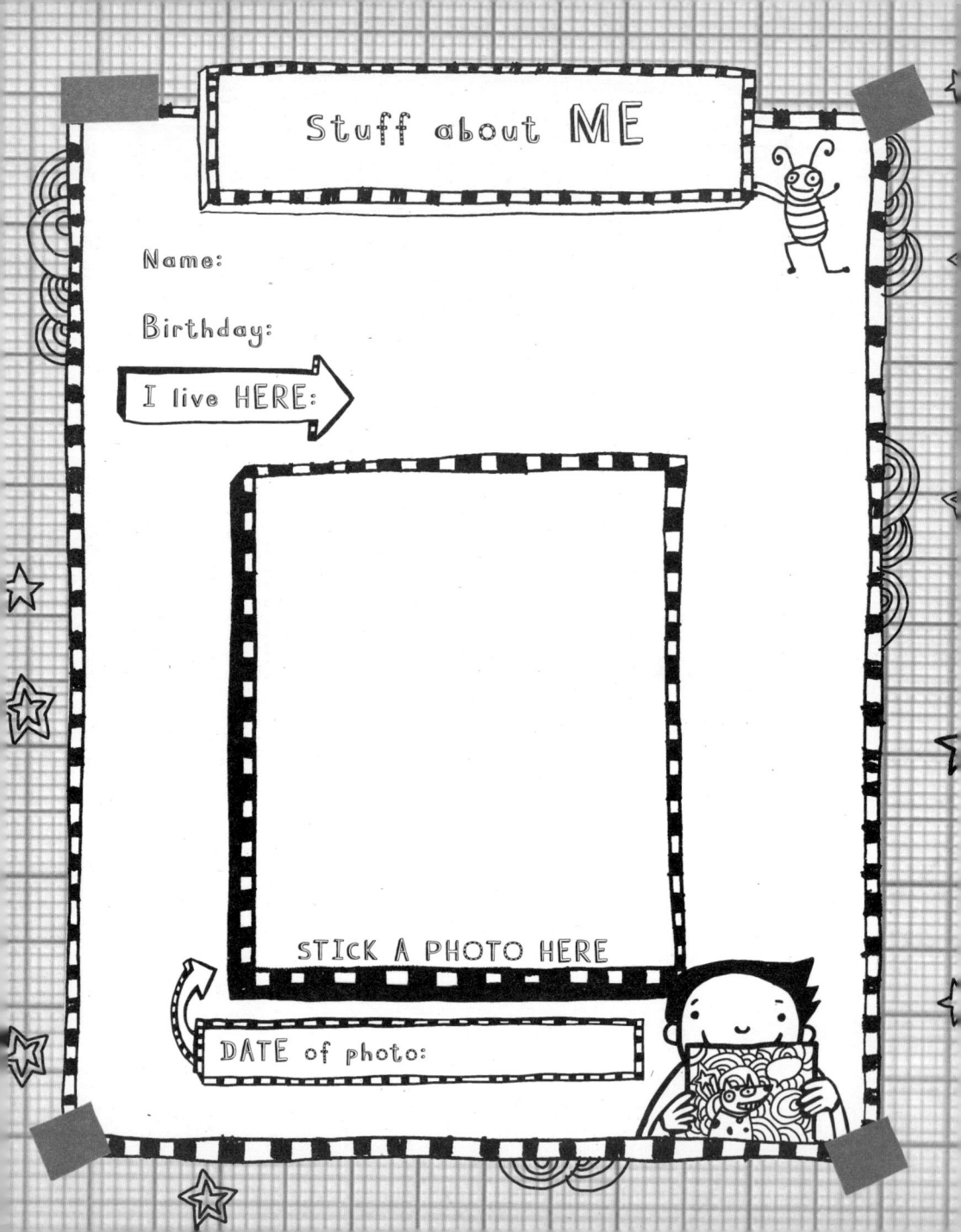

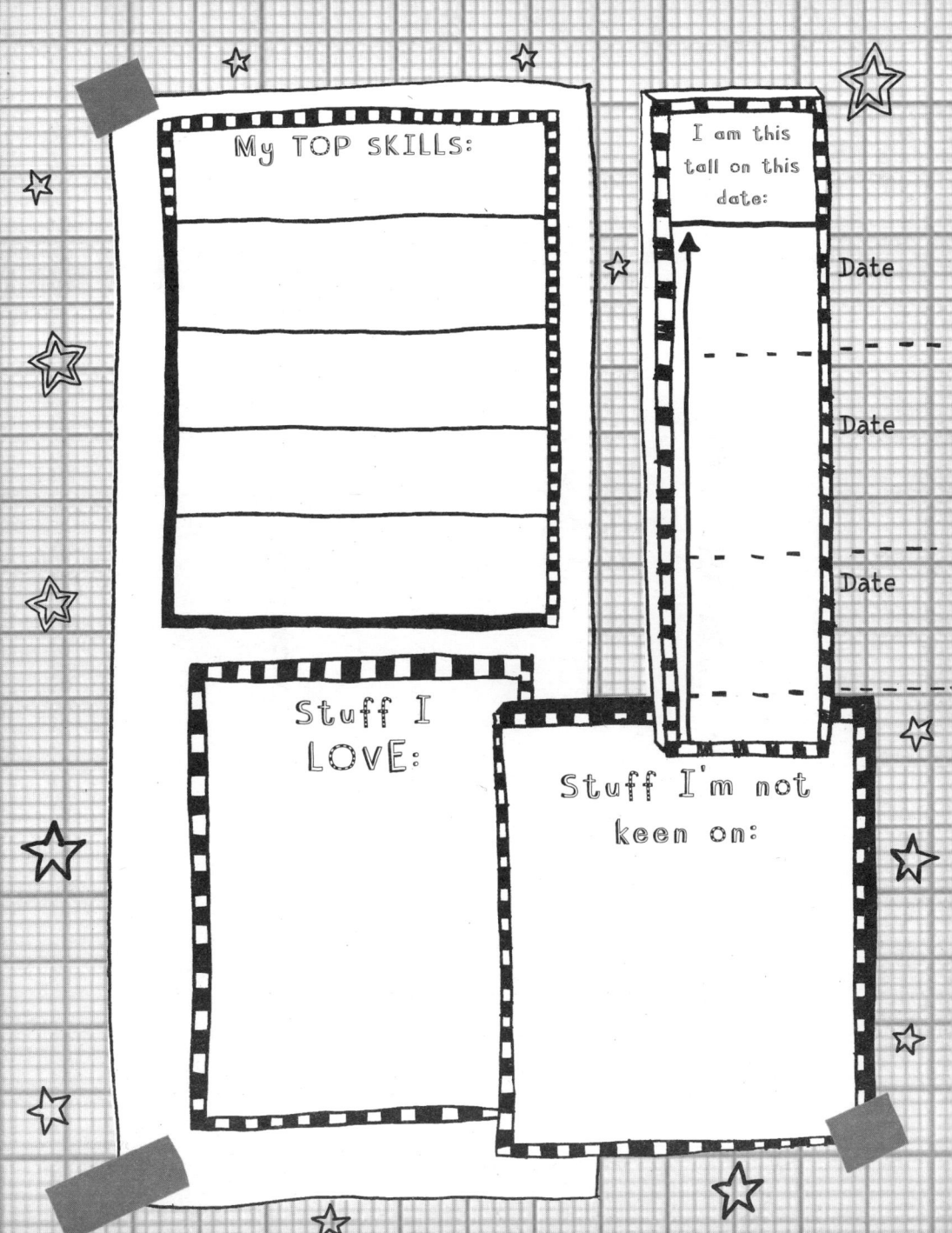

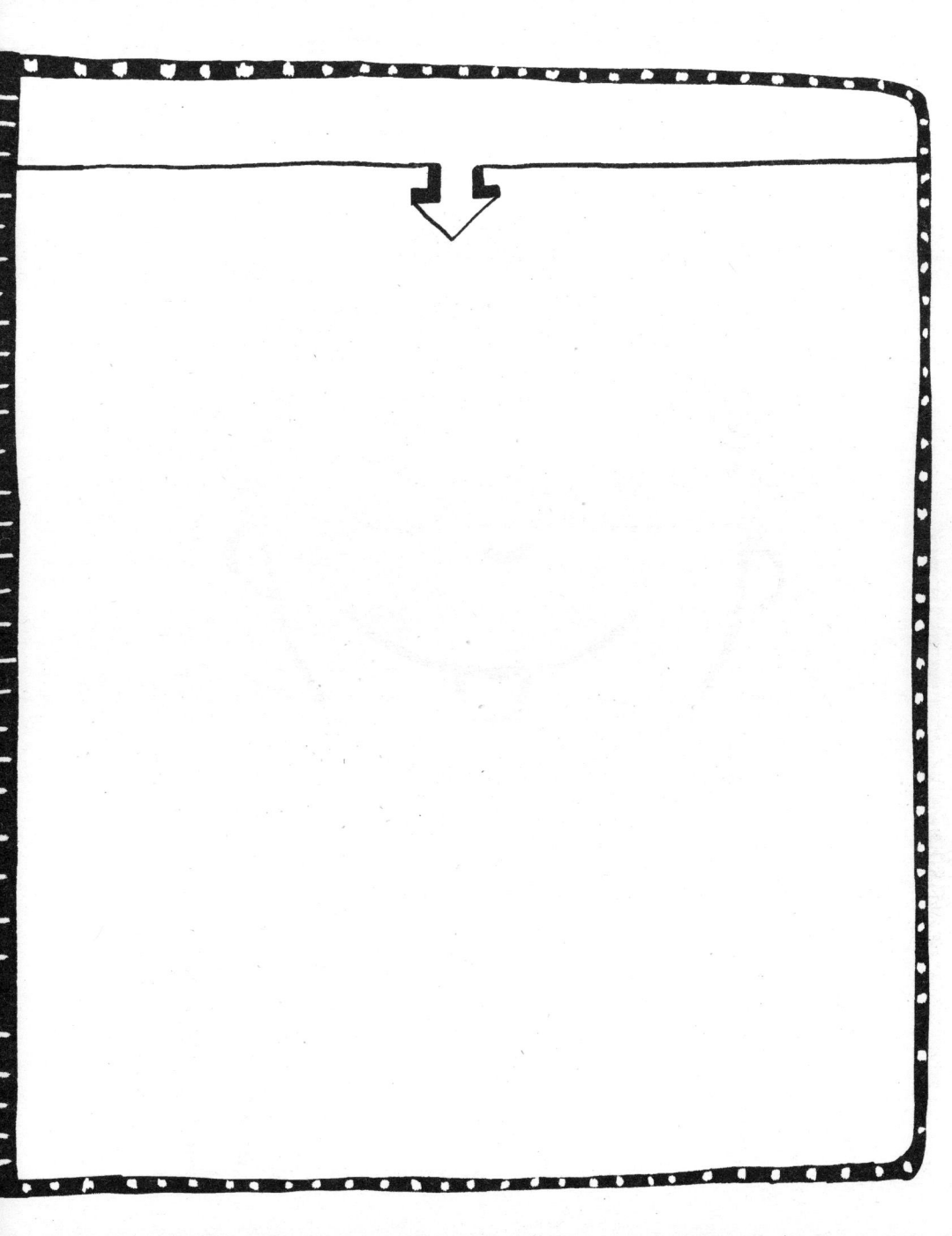

Write your name and DRAW lovely lines all round it.

Very HEAVY Triangle

Draw what is holding it up. →

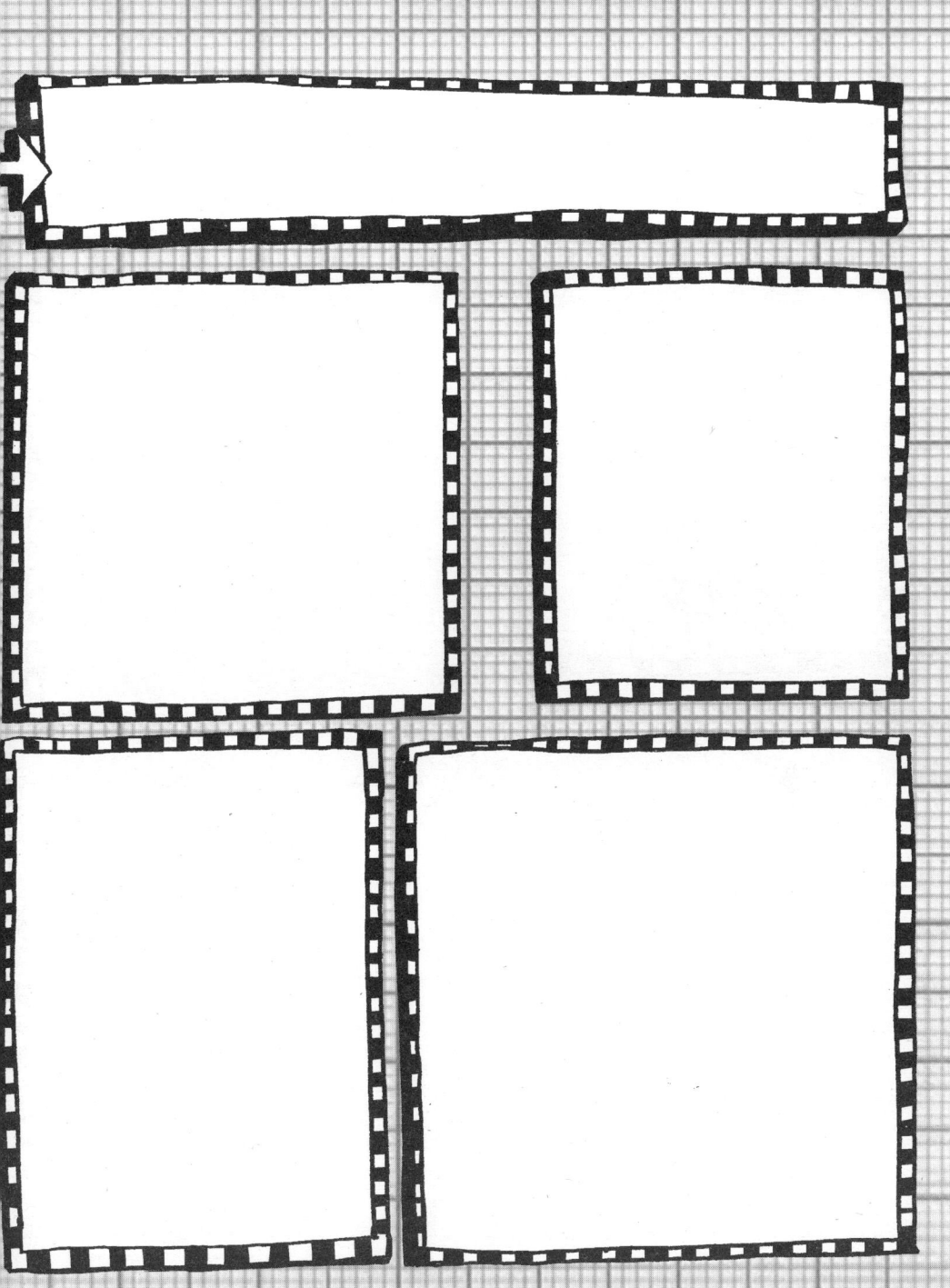

Test your pens out here.

Pens at the ready!

Fill
this page with
lots of swirls.

FILL these pages with rubbings from coins or flat interesting objects. Pop the coin under the page and use the side of a pencil to rub over the top.

SPRING

Trees, Shoes and Tiny Warblers

Here's my face when Mr Fullerman says...

 There's been a change of plan. It's such a beautiful SPRING DAY, I'd like to do a different lesson and take you all outside.

Which sounds EXCITING!

Looking around, I'm not the only one who's happy about the change of plan.

"We're going to be discovering the WONDER of plants and incredible wildlife that's all around us."

This lesson is getting BETTER and BETTER. Sounds like we're going on a TRIP!

"SIR, are you taking us to a **wildlife park?**" Florence asks.

"Can we feed the animals? Do they like cheese?"  Norman wants to know.

Mr Fullerman gives him one of his LOOKS

(which means ... NO).

"It's **SO** much better than that.
We're going outside to ...

the school grounds!

Mr Fullerman tries to make it sound good, but we all know a **wildlife park** is MUCH better than the school grounds.

Norman expresses his feelings loudly.
"AAAAAAAAwwwwwwwwwwwwwwwwwwwwww!"

You'd be SURPRISED by the EXCITING wildlife and plants that are RIGHT in front of you.

There's probably an INCREDIBLE insect that's flying past <u>this</u> window right NOW.

Everyone turns to look out of the window...

Caretaker Stan is walking past. He's not sure why we're staring at him — so he WAVES.
We wave back.

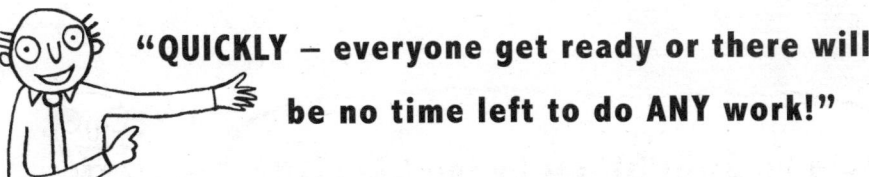

"QUICKLY — everyone get ready or there will be no time left to do ANY work!"

Mr Fullerman says, trying to hurry us all up.

Some kids take that as a challenge to move even ...
SLOWER.

(Mr Fullerman is WISE to this trick.)

"Solid, WHY are you holding a chair?" Mr Fullerman asks.

"To sit on outside, sir."

(Good thinking, Solid.)

Everyone starts picking up chairs because this is a very good idea.

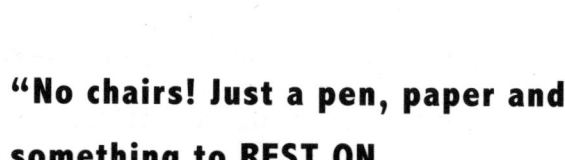

"No chairs! Just a pen, paper and something to REST ON...

Not a TABLE, Brad," Mr Fullerman says.

He's sighing a lot now.

We start to line up and then follow Mr Fullerman down the corridor.

For some reason, Norman keeps jumping up and down.

I can see Mrs Mumble walking towards us. She's SMILING at first, but the closer she gets, the more worried she looks.

"Did I miss a fire alarm, Mr Fullerman?"

"No, Mrs Mumble — it's just such a LOVELY SPRING day that we're going outside to do our work and study the interesting plants and LOCAL wildlife on the school grounds."

Mrs Mumble seems pleased about that.

"HOW fantastic! I heard on the radio this morning that there's been sightings of a VERY RARE and beautiful bird called a Tiny Golden Warbler," she tells us.

"It hasn't been seen in OAKFIELD TOWN for over **TWENTY YEARS** and it's suddenly **BACK**."

How INTERESTING!

Mr Fullerman says.
"Hands up if you've ever seen a picture of a Tiny Golden Warbler before,"
Mrs Mumble asks us hopefully.
Norman puts his hand
up quickly.

Wonderful! Do tell everyone what's SO special about the bird, Norman.

"I just need the TOILET PLEASE."

While Mr Fullerman sends Norman off, Mrs Mumble describes what the bird looks like.

It's very small BUT with **GLORIOUS** bright yellow feathers on its head that look like a little crown. And if you're **LUCKY** enough to see one – it's a magical moment. So **KEEP** a **LOOK-OUT** as you never know. Imagine the **RARE** bird coming to our school! I'd put it in the school newsletter for sure!

"We'll try our best, Mrs Mumble. Won't we, class?" Mr Fullerman says.

We sort of reply "YES" but it doesn't sound like anyone is *that* excited about a bird. (If we were going to a **wildlife park** that might be different.)

"I'll probably SPOT the bird as I've got VERY good EYESIGHT," Marcus tells me.

"LOOK - there it is!"
I point to the window again.

"WHERE? LET ME SEE!"

Marcus shouts.

"Made you look..." I LAUGH.
"You'll scare it away if you talk THAT LOUDLY, Marcus!" AMY tells him.

"I won't - I knew Tom was only joking," Marcus says.

(He didn't.)

Shocked bird

Mr Fullerman heads outside and STOPS at a large plant pot and waits for us to catch up.

There are a few of these pots in the school grounds that have nice flowers and plants in.

They used to have pebbles too, but when the stone-collection CRAZE started, kids kept taking them and now there's none left.

"Gather round, EVERYONE. OK – does anyone know what THIS type of plant is called?"
Mr Fullerman wants to know.

Ha! Ha! Ha!

"A DEAD plant?

I say, and everyone LAUGHS.

"I don't think it's DEAD, Tom. If you look CLOSELY, you'll see the tiny buds about to **BURST** into life on this CAMELLIA plant."

We all move forward.

"It still looks ... dead, sir," **AMY** says.

Then Mr Fullerman accidentally **SNAPS** a branch OFF (because it's dead).

"OH! You might be right. Shall we see what's in the SOIL instead? There's always plenty of bugs and creatures to be found if you dig down a little deeper—" he tells us, and starts to move the soil with the branch.

"What have we got HERE?"

Mr Fullerman finds something and holds up ...

 a bottle top.
"THIS should be in the BIN."

Then Pansy find another one.

"Hey, sir, I've found a RED bottle top!"

"I've got a BLUE one!" Leroy adds.

"Here's a GREEN one – maybe that's why the plant died?" Marcus suggests.

"We should start collecting bottle tops instead of STONES. They make excellent badges too," I point out, and everyone starts searching for MORE bottle tops.

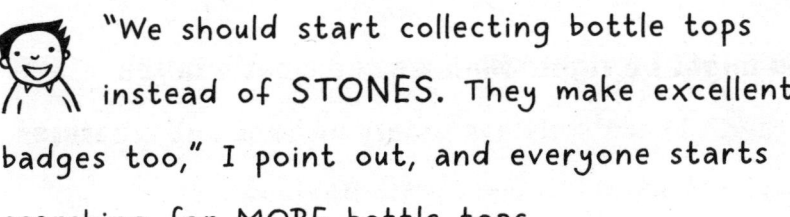

"No one should be putting bottle tops IN the PLANT POTS. Come along – follow me over to that BIG TREE. I'll tell you some interesting FACTS about leaves."

(As Mr Fullerman heads off, I find a red bottle top.)

I'm so busy looking at my bottle top I don't notice that everyone's left me. **Mr Fullerman** is now standing under the **BIG TREE** trying to get the class **EXCITED** about leaves.

(I'm not sure THIS is the lesson **Mr Fullerman** was planning.)

"This is a HORNBEAM tree that's been in the school grounds for a LONG time — it's quite old."

"Is it as old as you, sir?" Solid asks.

 **"OLDER,"** he says, and Solid goes "Ooohhhhh..." like he's shocked.

"This is a DECIDUOUS tree.

Does anyone know what that means?"

"It's a TREE ... that's DANGEROUS.

SIR ... an ANT'S crawled up my leg!"

Norman says while wiggling his leg around.

Julia Morton puts up her hand to tell us,

"Trees CAN be dangerous.

I fell out of a tree and broke my arm, sir."

 "I've done that,"

Norman adds.

(So have I – but it was mostly the doughnut's fault.*)

"It's not dangerous – it means the leaves

fall OFF the branches in the autumn,"

Mr Fullerman explains ... slowly.

* See my book *Random Acts of Fun*.

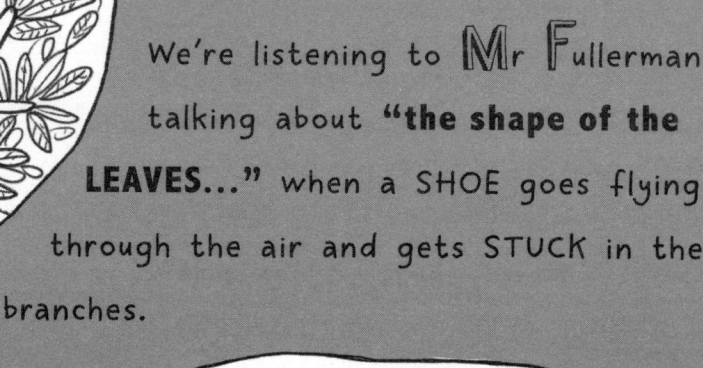

We're listening to Mr Fullerman talking about **"the shape of the LEAVES..."** when a SHOE goes flying through the air and gets STUCK in the branches.

> Who did that?

he shouts.

It's not hard to guess as Brad's only wearing one shoe and a sock.

"Sorry, sir, I was trying to knock that branch down so I could get a closer look at the LEAVES."

"Of course you were, Brad — why <u>else</u> would you THROW your shoe into the tree?"

Mr Fullerman sounds fed up.
We watch as he tries to REACH UP and grab it — but he's too short.
Then Mr Fullerman SHAKES the tree.
But that doesn't work either.

Next, he throws his CLIPBOARD right into the branches ... where it stays.

"Sir, we could all throw our shoes up together — that might work,"

I suggest.

"**No,**" Mr Fullerman tells us.

"I'm going to get a BALL. Everyone carry on filling in your worksheets."

The first thing Brad does is throw his other shoe...

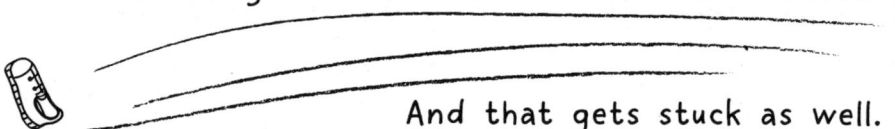

And that gets stuck as well.

"Aww - now I've got no shoes," Brad complains.

 "Mr Fullerman told you not to," Marcus reminds him.

I sit down on the grass and start to answer the questions.

1. DESCRIBE SOME OF THE PLANTS YOU'VE SEEN:
   Mostly dead twigs.

2. WHAT DID YOU FIND IN THE SOIL?
   A nice collection of different-coloured BOTTLE TOPS!

Mr Fullerman returns with a tennis ball.

"**Keep clear, everyone,**" he says.

The rest of the class sit on the grass and enjoy watching Mr Fullerman do underarm throws to knock the shoes and clipboard out of the tree.

"**This won't take long,**" he tells us.

(This is not true.)

He's still throwing the ball when AMY says, "Sir, Mrs Mumble is waving at us from the school office."

"I think she's trying to get your attention, sir," AMY lets him know.

Mrs Mumble's not just WAVING.

She's leaping around and looks very HAPPY!

"She's probably wondering why I'm throwing the ball into the tree," he tells us.

"It's OK, Mrs Mumble – I'm just trying to get my clipboard down!"

Mr Fullerman calls back, and gives her the THUMBS UP.

"I'll explain LATER, Mrs Mumble!"

"**Brad, I'll ask Caretaker Stan if he can get your shoe down now,**" he adds.

 "My SHOES, sir – they've both got stuck," Brad tells him

Mr Fullerman sighs.

I haven't seen many CREATURES or bugs but it's lovely being in the SUNSHINE, ☼ drawing the tree.

Marcus isn't happy though – he sat on a wet patch of grass and now he's complaining.

You'll dry out in the sun ... eventually.

I tell him.

AWWWW.

Back in the classroom, Mrs Mumble is THERE waiting for us.

"Hello, Mrs Mumble – is everything OK?"
Mr Fullerman asks, as this is UNUSUAL.

She's <u>still</u> HAPPY and ever so EXCITED to tell us:

"Wasn't that the MOST wonderful sight? I couldn't believe MY EYES!"

 "I was trying to get my clipboard down from the tree – and Brad's shoe," Mr Fullerman explains.

"My SHOES, sir, and now my socks are wet," Brad adds.

"And I've got a wet patch too," Marcus grumbles.

"Didn't you see the Tiny Golden Warbler? It was IN the TREE and flying around you!

That RARE special bird was HERE IN OAKFIELD SCHOOL! You did see it, didn't you, Mr Fullerman? ANYone?" Mrs Mumble asks us.

Norman puts up his hand.

"Did you see it, NORMAN?"
Mr Fullerman asks.

"No, sir, I just need the toilet."

Mr Fullerman sighs loudly again.
"It's nearly breaktime, Norman, you can wait. I can't believe we MISSED the RARE bird, Mrs Mumble. That's so disappointing."

"And I thought your class were busy drawing the tiny bird up in the tree," Mrs Mumble tells him.

While Mr Fullerman and Mrs Mumble chat about missing out on seeing the Tiny Golden Warbler, Norman walks over to the window and says...

"Hey, look at that!"

We look out of the window.

And THERE on the GRASS is ... the Tiny Golden Warbler. It really is BRIGHT YELLOW with a crown of feathers on its head.

"Mr Fullerman! Mr Fullerman! It's the bird!"

Marcus calls out SO LOUDLY the bird hears him and flies OFF.

"**Where is it?**" Mr Fullerman asks.

"You were too slow, sir," Marcus says.

"You were too LOUD, Marcus," AMY reminds him.

Then I say, "Don't worry, sir, it'll come back – in twenty years."

And Mr Fullerman smiles, then sighs. Sigh...

The GOOD NEWS is...

Mr Fullerman and everyone else who missed out on seeing the RARE bird get to read all about it in the **SPECIAL EDITION** of the **OAKFIELD SCHOOL NEWSLETTER** that Mrs Mumble has put together.

Our class has an excellent **NATURE table display** too. There's TREE drawings, different-shaped leaves, dead twigs, bottle tops and, best of all, pictures of the Tiny Golden Warbler. And I even made my bottle top into a very nice badge. Lessons outside in spring are the best.

SPACE FOR YOUR OWN STORY

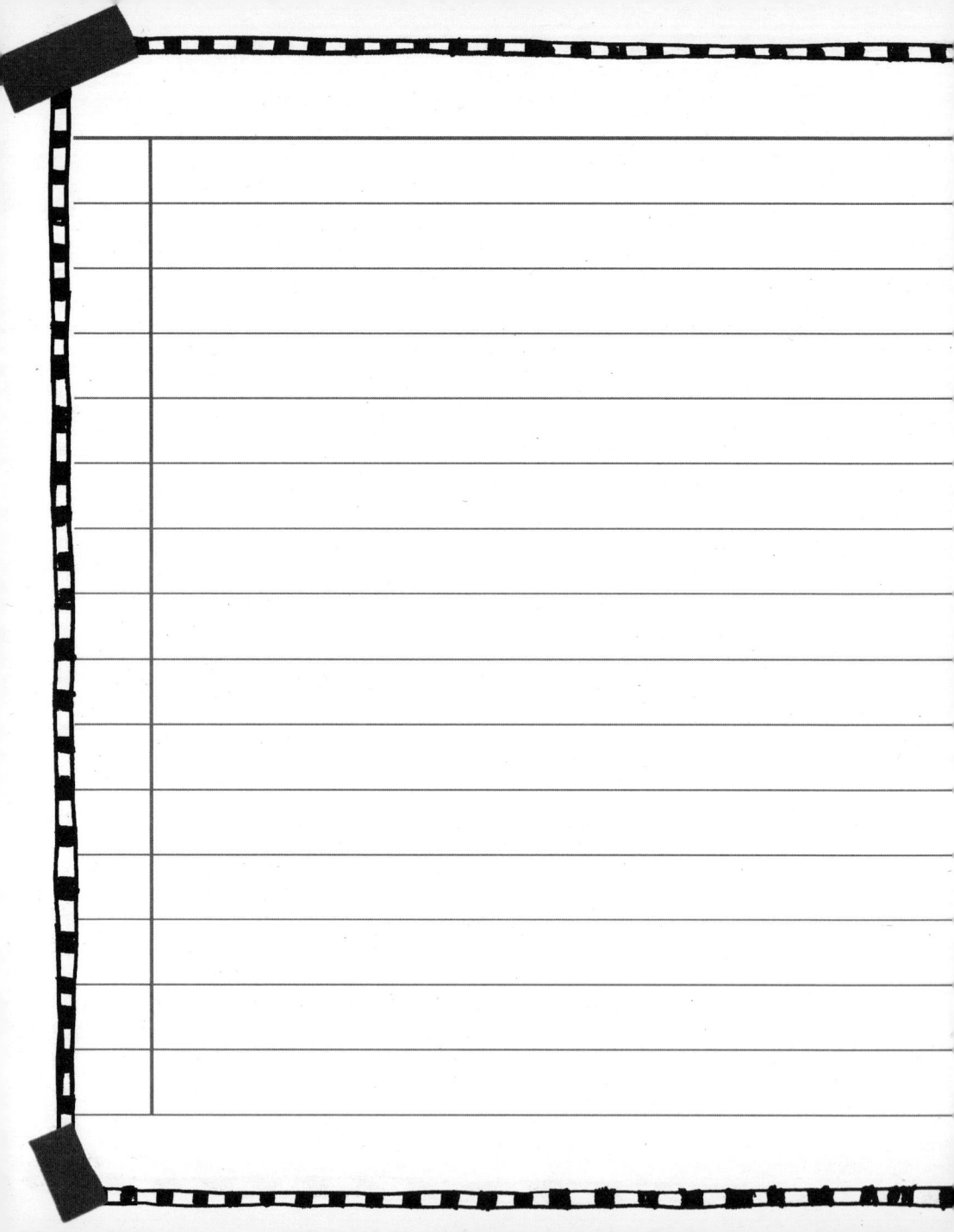

DRAW PICTuREs to GO with YOuR STORY

Bring these plants BACK to life.

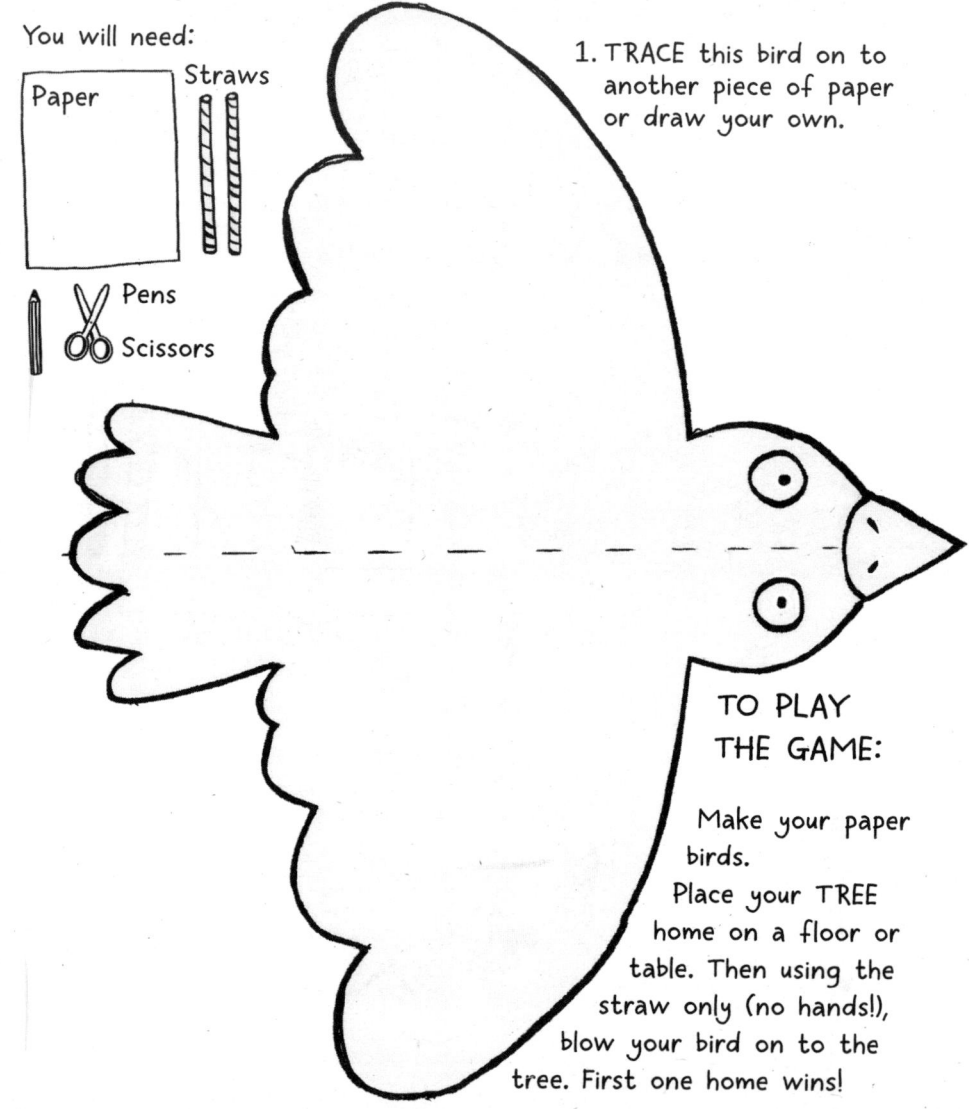

2. Once you've drawn your bird, colour it in and fold it in half.

3. Cut out the bird. BE careful with scissors!

4. Your bird's ready!

5. Then draw a tree for its HOME on another piece of paper. Place it on the floor or on a table.

Then get ready...
Get set...
GO!

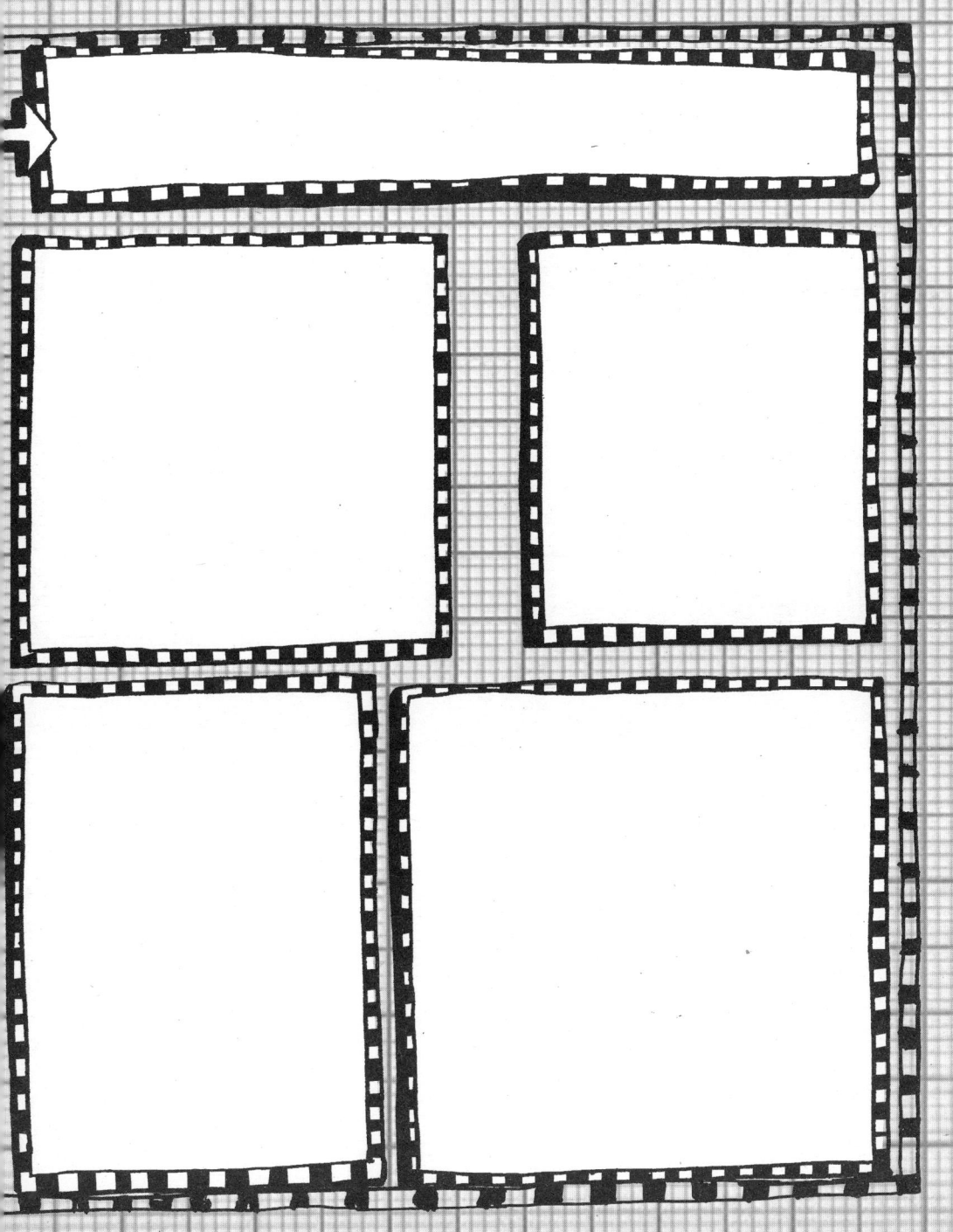

What's the sound under ground?

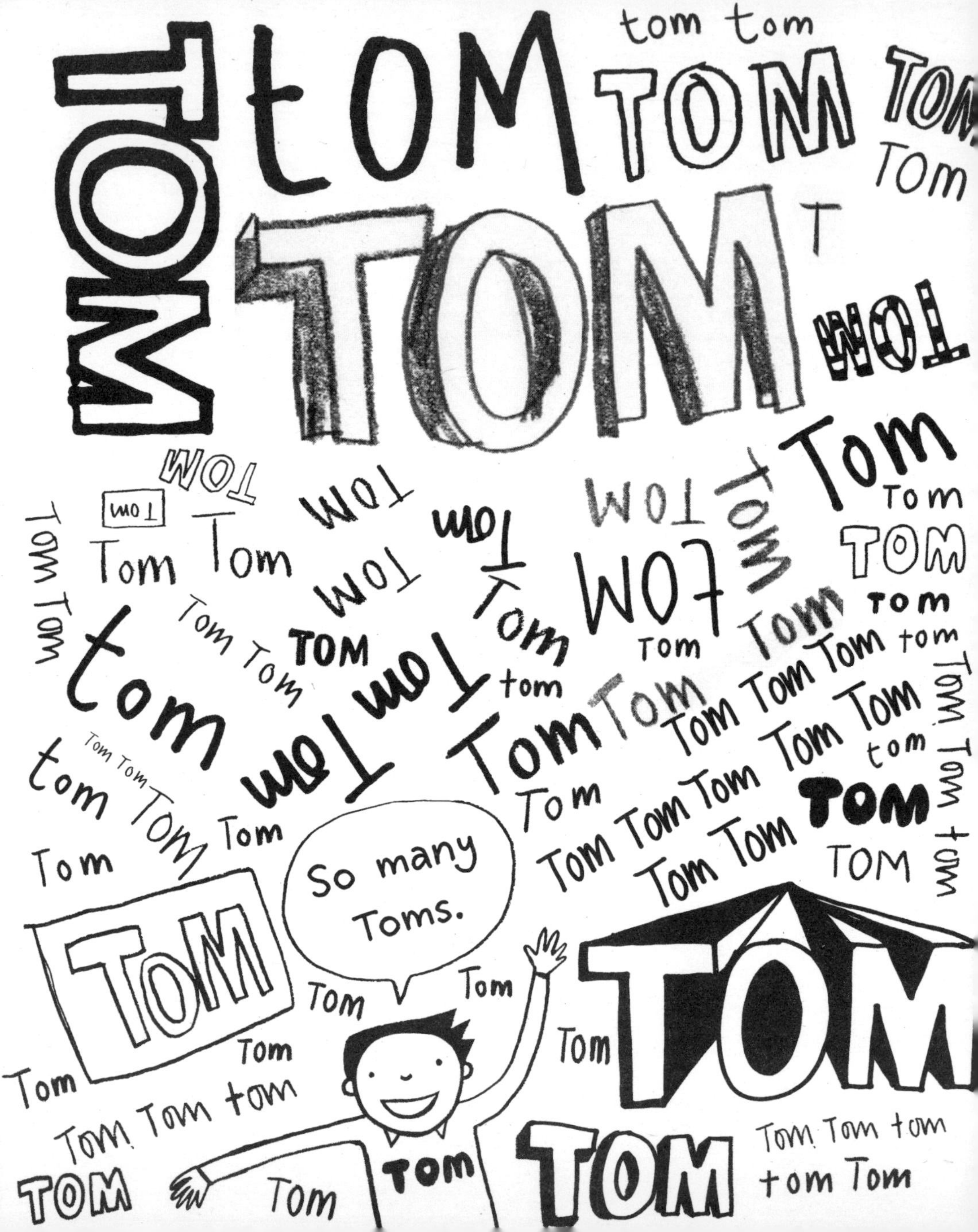
So many Toms.

WRITE your NAME LOADS OF DIFFERENT WAYS and FILL THE PAGE.

ADD MORE WIGGLY LINES.

JUST ADD

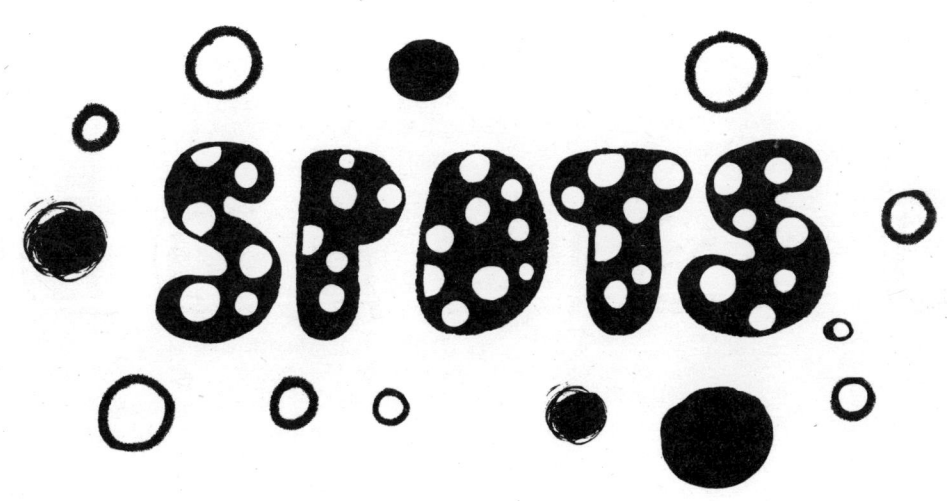

squidges

EXPERIMENT with paint and different brushes.

swirls

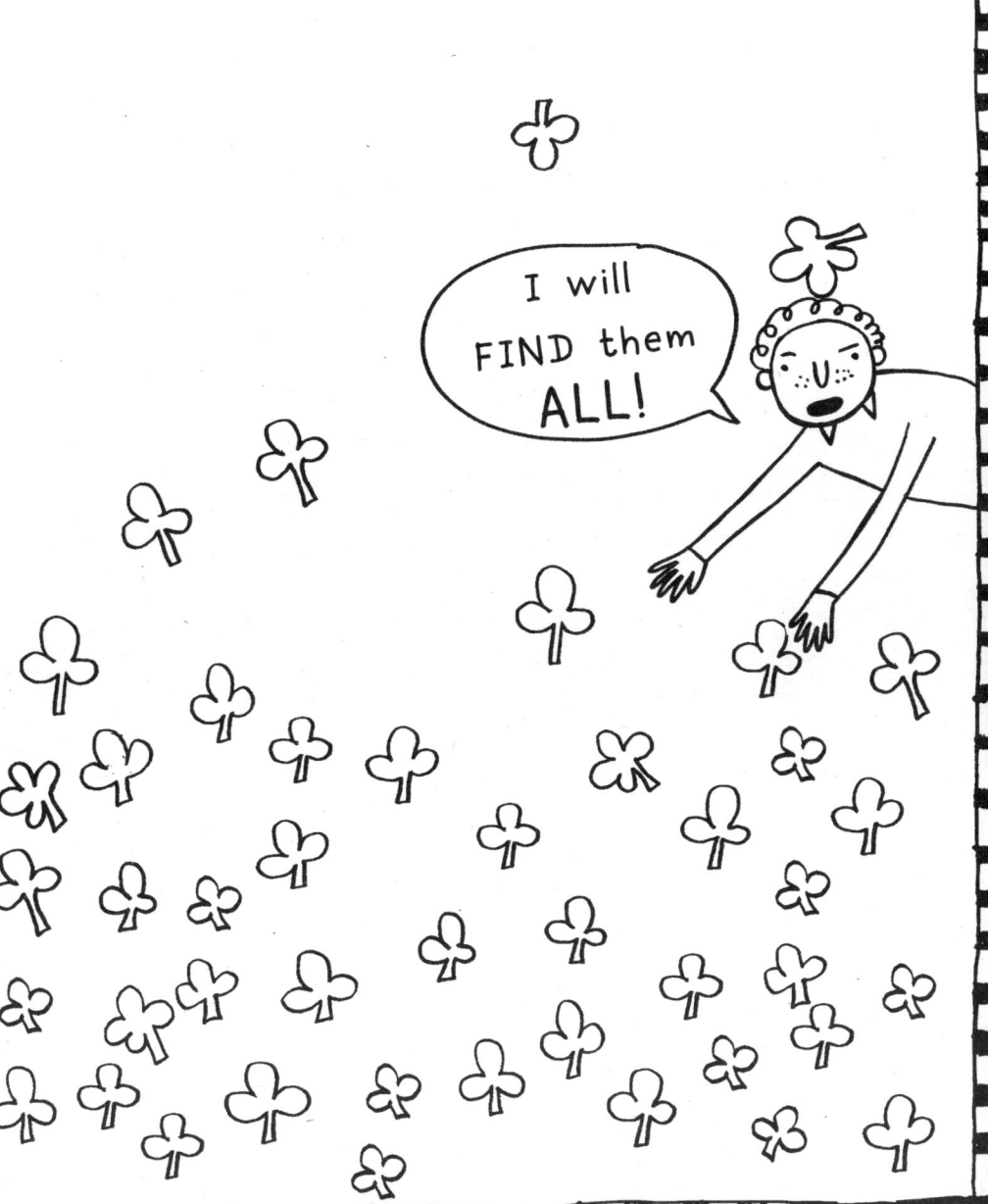

ARTY STUFF

Make a PEN holder

You will need:
- Air-drying clay
- Pens
- Paint to decorate

1. Shape your clay into a rectangle. Make it deep enough to hold the pens.

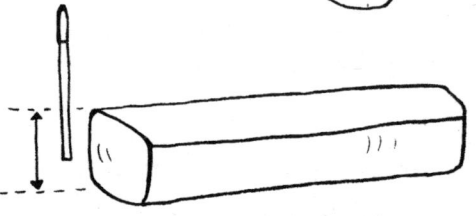

2. Use water to smooth the edges with your fingers.

smooth smooth

3. Then take the END of the pen you want to put in the holder. →

Gently push it into the clay to make a hole.

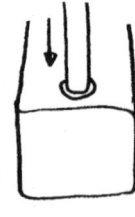

4. Space the holes along the rectangle. If it moves out of shape - pat it back into a rectangle and re-do the hole.

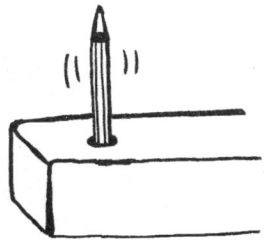

Let it dry completely. Be patient!

5. Decorate with paint, pens, or both. Let it dry again.

6. Put your pens in your new pen holder!

I'm sitting in the garden when I hear MUSIC.

Not just any old MUSIC.

It's the SOUND of the ICE-CREAM VAN.

I could do with a lolly or an ice cream as it's a really HOT day (and I like ice cream).

Yes!

I run into the house as *FAST* as I can because the ice-cream van doesn't hang around. You have to be *QUICK*.

𝔻ad's on the phone and can't talk. I let him know this is an **EMERGENCY** and act out

"Ice cream from the ice-cream van" so he knows what I'm asking.

(Go and ask your mum...) he tells me, and points upstairs.

I go and find her *FAST.*

(The music keeps playing, which means the van is still there, but for how long?)

3 mins gone. There's NO time to waste.

Mum's in the bathroom.

So I KNOCK LOUDLY and call out:

(Mum! Mum! The ice-cream van's here! Can we get ice cream?)

I don't know where Delia is, and Dad's still on the phone.

This is NOT ideal, but I can't waste any more time.

Now Mum wants an ice cream too.

The quickest way to find Delia is to SHOUT...

* A 99 is a type of ice cream in a cone with a chocolate flake.

Delia doesn't answer.

=I BARGE into her room but she's not there either. "DELIA!" I call out.

Then I RUN BACK downstairs, where I FIND her sitting in the NEW swivel chair with her headphones on. She looks very relaxed until I SPIN her to get her attention.

"DELIA! Mum said you can come with me to BUY ICE CREAM from the ICE-CREAM VAN — QUICKLY!"

"STOP SPINNING ME, TOM!"

(At least she's listening now...)

"Calm down, Tom – it's only ice cream."

"It's NOT just ice cream. It's 99's with flakes and sprinkles!"

(That gets Delia moving – everyone likes 99's.)

Outside, I can SEE the van is parked at the end of our road – AND there's no queue.

Which is BRILLIANT!

As we get closer ...

the van suddenly ...

DRIVES OFF!

"Oh dear! Never mind, Tom."

"NO! Come back!"

This is a **DISASTER!** It doesn't even have its music on – which means it's NOT going to stop again. I watch the van disappear ... sadly.

Delia doesn't seem that bothered.

"You were SO slow – we missed the ice-cream van. It's gone now."

"Don't blame me. You shouldn't have spent so much time spinning me in the chair!" Delia says.

It's a long slow walk home for me... ☹

All the time I'm getting hotter. If ONLY I had something to cool me down, like an ice cream ... or an ice lolly.

Delia gets home before me, because I keep hoping the van will SUDDENLY come back and I'm listening out for the music, but there's nothing.

I might as well go and SIT in the NEW chair and have a SPIN.

This will CHEER me up and take my mind off missing out on a 99 ice cream – a bit.

(Sigh...)

No ice cream = hot face

BUT I can't even do THAT! Delia's sitting in the chair and looking all comfortable and SMUG.

THEN I notice...

She's ONLY EATING AN ICE LOLLY!

"HEY, WHERE DID YOU GET THAT FROM?" I want to know.

"I MADE THEM YESTERDAY – do you want one?" Delia says unexpectedly, and hands ME a lolly.

"Have you licked it?" I check, because it's the sort of thing I'd do.

"No, Tom. Don't take it then," she says.

"I'll have it – thanks, Delia."

I taste the lolly carefully, just in case.

"What do you think?" Delia wants to know.

"It's OK – not as good as a 99, but not bad," I tell her. (Which is TRUE.)

"Can I sit in the chair now?"

"No, and don't spin me," she says, which is a mistake.

(Of course I'm going to spin her.)

Had enough?

SPACE FOR YOUR OWN STORY

DRAW PICTURES to GO with YOUR STORY

DRAW what Delia is looking at in her glasses.

DRAW a CLOSE-UP of someone you know with glasses.

Make Fruit-Juice Lollies

You will need:

- Ice-cube tray or lolly mould
- Straws or wooden sticks
- Fruit juice
- A jug (if you have one)

1. Use a lolly mould or make tiny lollies with an ice-cube tray. Pour the fruit juice into the mould or tray. Use a jug if it's easier.

2. Pop in the freezer until almost frozen. (Check it after an hour or so.) Then take them out and pop the stick or straw into the juice. Put back in the freezer until fully frozen.

3. Now enjoy your LOLLY!

Draw Your Favourite Animals

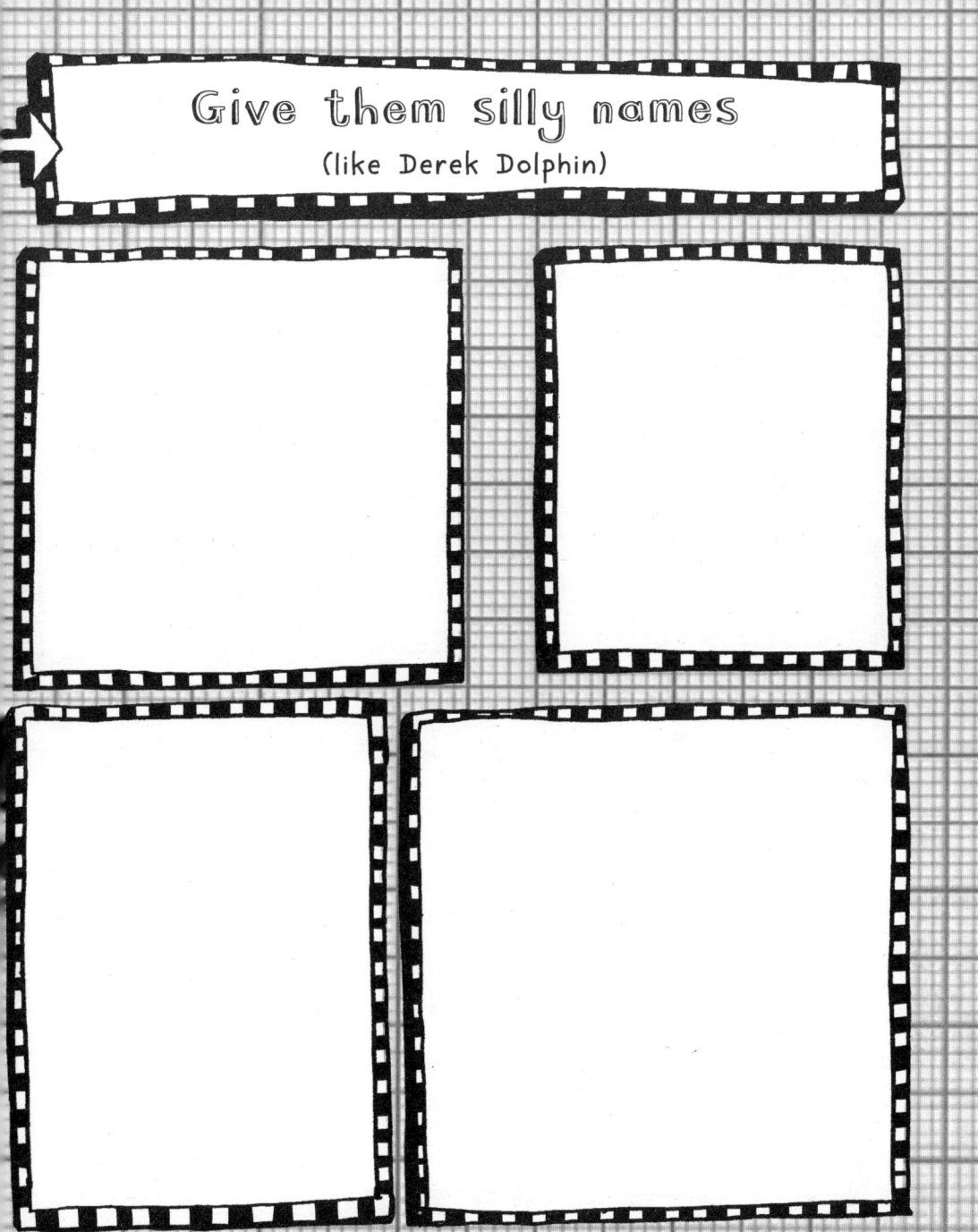

UPCYCLE an old T-shirt

You will need:
An old T-shirt    A4 paper ▢   Fabric pens or paint 🖍️

Pencil ✏️   Black pen 🖊️   Rubber

1. This is a GREAT way to make an OLD tee look AMAZING again! Take your T-shirt and cover up a stain or add doodles to the old design.

 Stain

Old design → Add more doodles. → New design

2.
Draw your design in black pen on A4 paper.

3.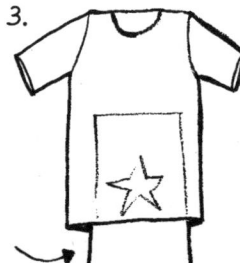
Next, slip it inside your T-shirt.

4.
Now use your fabric pens or paint to draw your design on to your T-shirt.

Trace this T-shirt and use it to work out your design.

5. Follow the FABRIC pens or paint instructions to FIX the design. Do get a grown-up to help you. Then wear your T-shirt and tell EVERYONE YOU designed it!

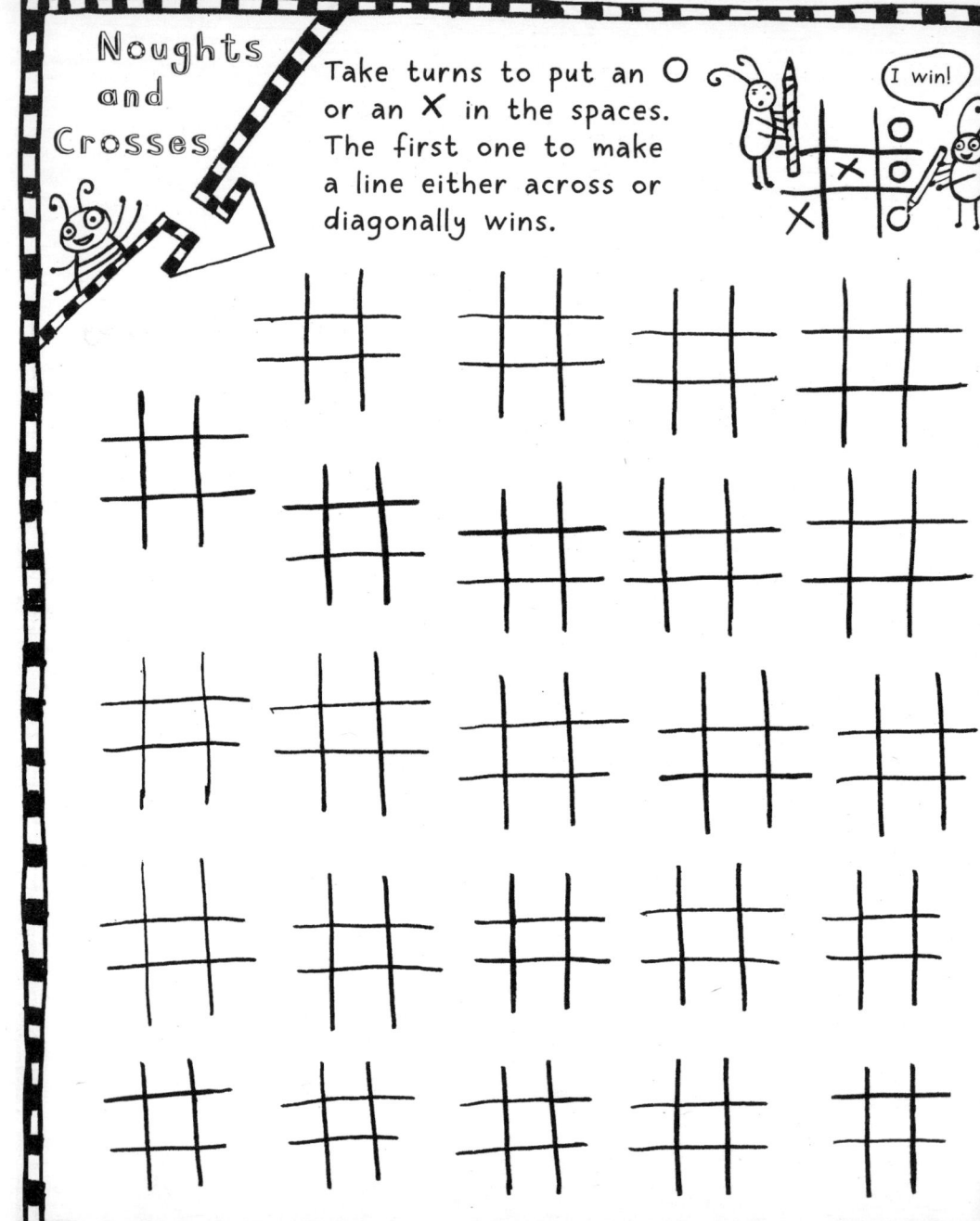

HOW TO PLAY BOXES

Take turns to draw lines connecting the dots to make boxes. The person who finishes the box CLAIMS it by putting their initial inside (or symbol). You have to take a turn, even if it means the other person will take the box. The winner has the most boxes when all the squares are completed.

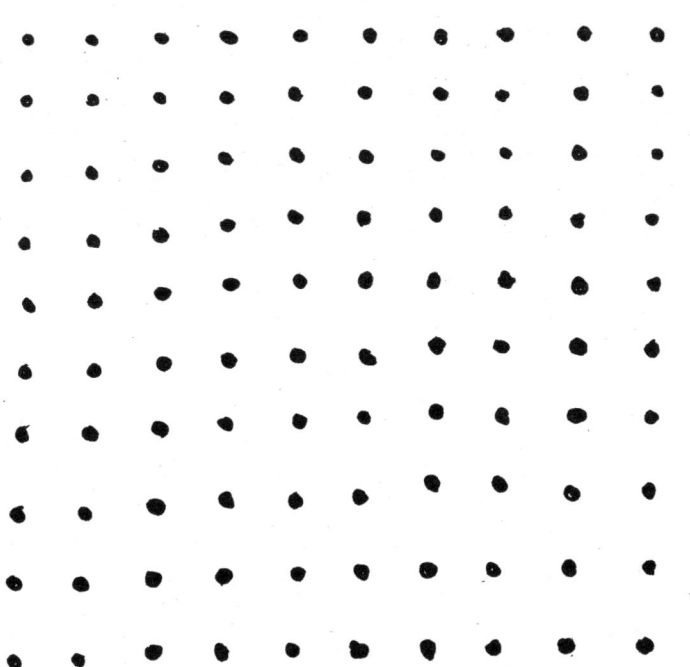

Colour in the squares
(if you have a spare ten hours...)

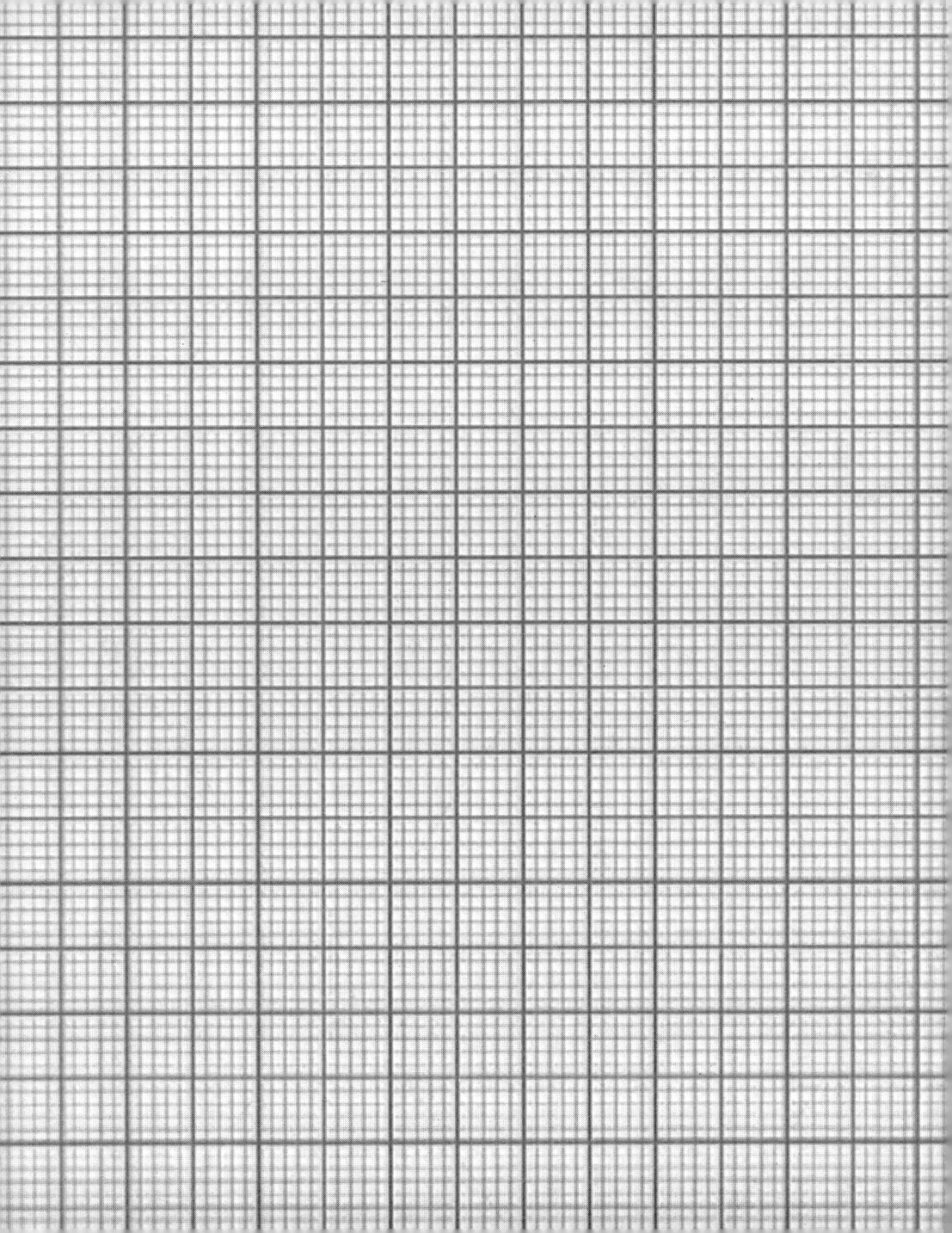

Get your friends to sign HERE

DRAW YOUR OWN COMIC SPREAD

SPACE FOR YOUR OWN STORY

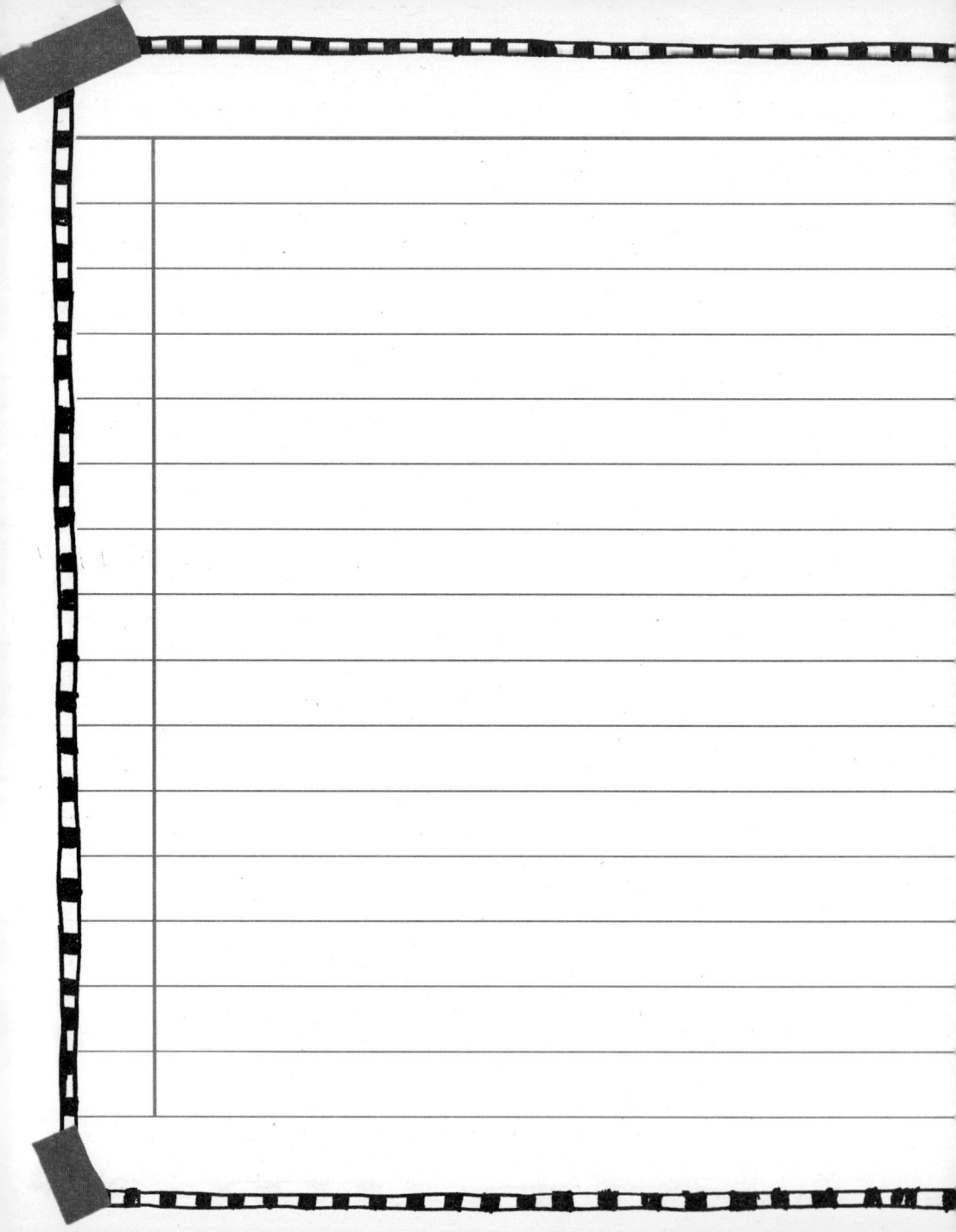

DRAW PICTUREs to GO with YOuR STORY

STICK INTERESTING LEAVES ON THESE PAGES.

PAPER-CHAIN GHOSTS
You will need: Thin A4 paper, scissors, glue, black pen.

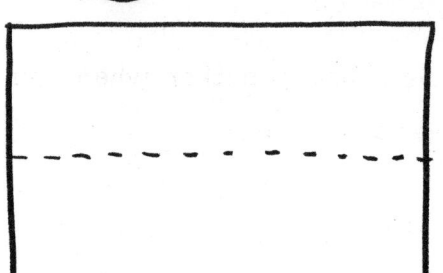
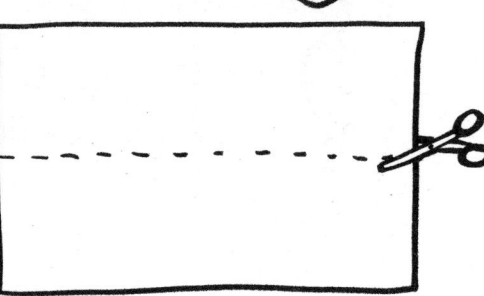

Take a sheet of A4 paper, fold it longways in half and carefully cut it along the fold.

Then glue the two halves together.

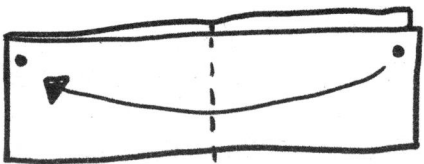

Fold the long paper in half. Then fold in half again, and again and again.

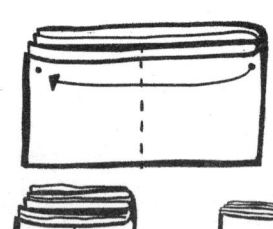

Folded side of the paper

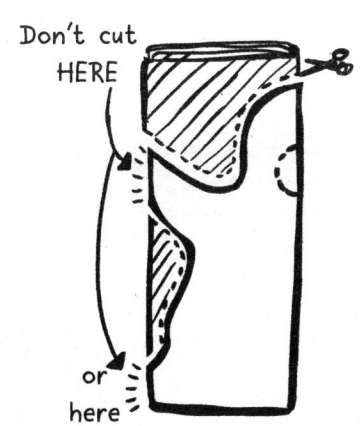

Draw half a ghost shape and half an open mouth on the folded side of the paper. Carefully cut through all the layers, taking <u>out</u> the shaded areas shown. The arms and bottom part of the ghost should still be linked together when you open UP the paper chain.

Be careful with scissors and always cut away from your fingers.

Next, DRAW on the EYES when you open the chain. To make a longer chain, stick more ghosts together.

By changing the shape you cut out, you can make snowmen, Christmas trees and lots of different types of paper chains. ENJOY!

tree

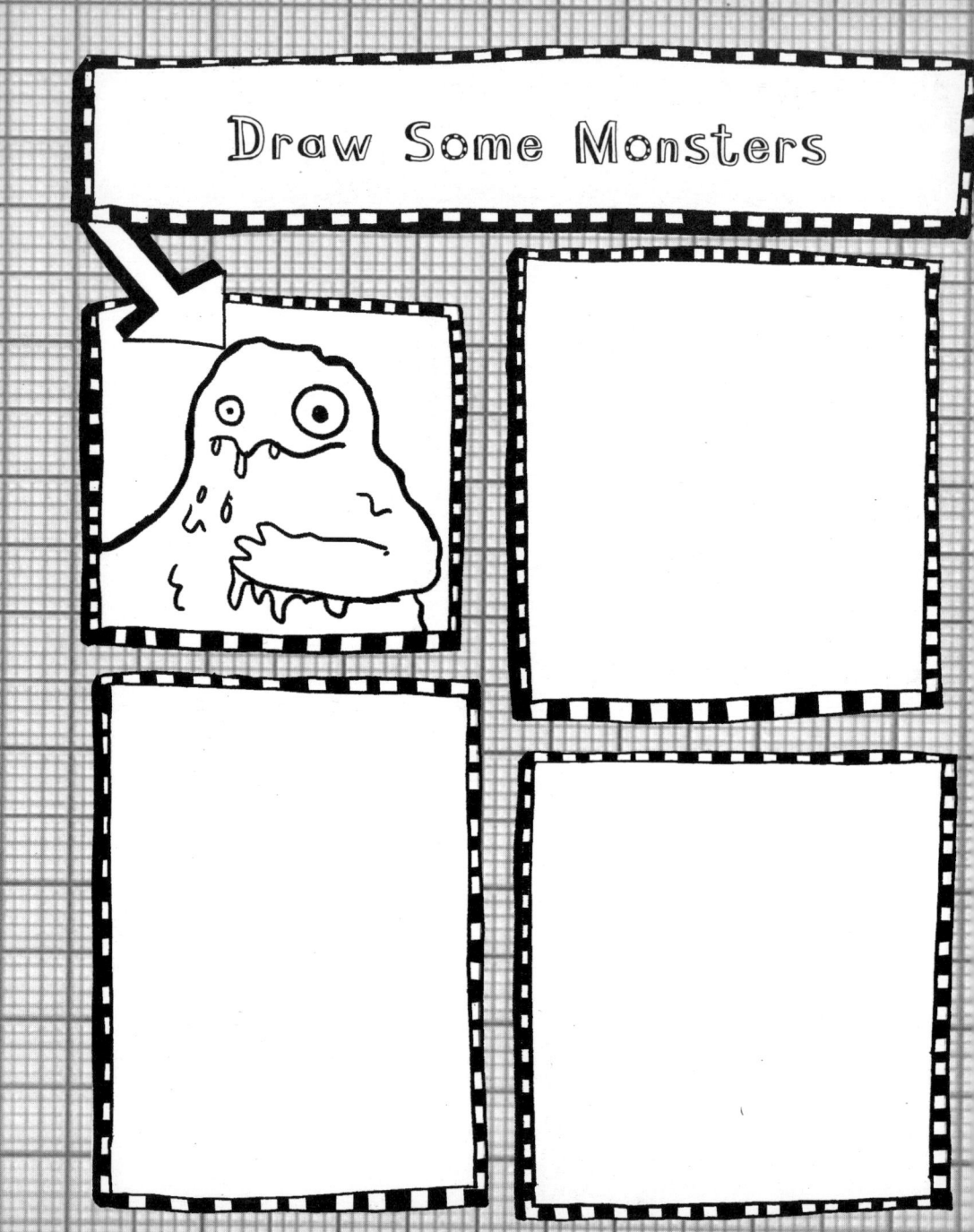

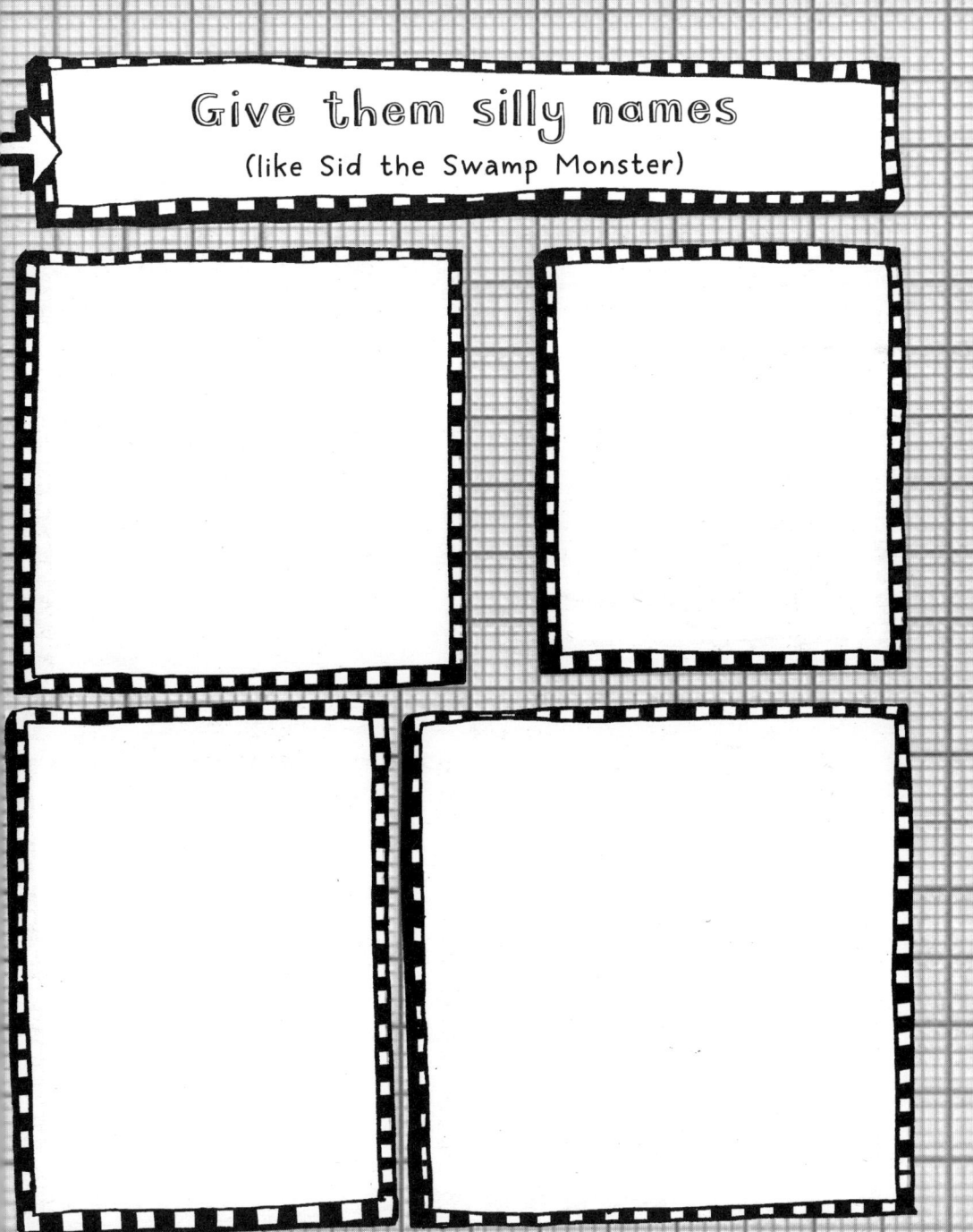

What ARE they SAYING?

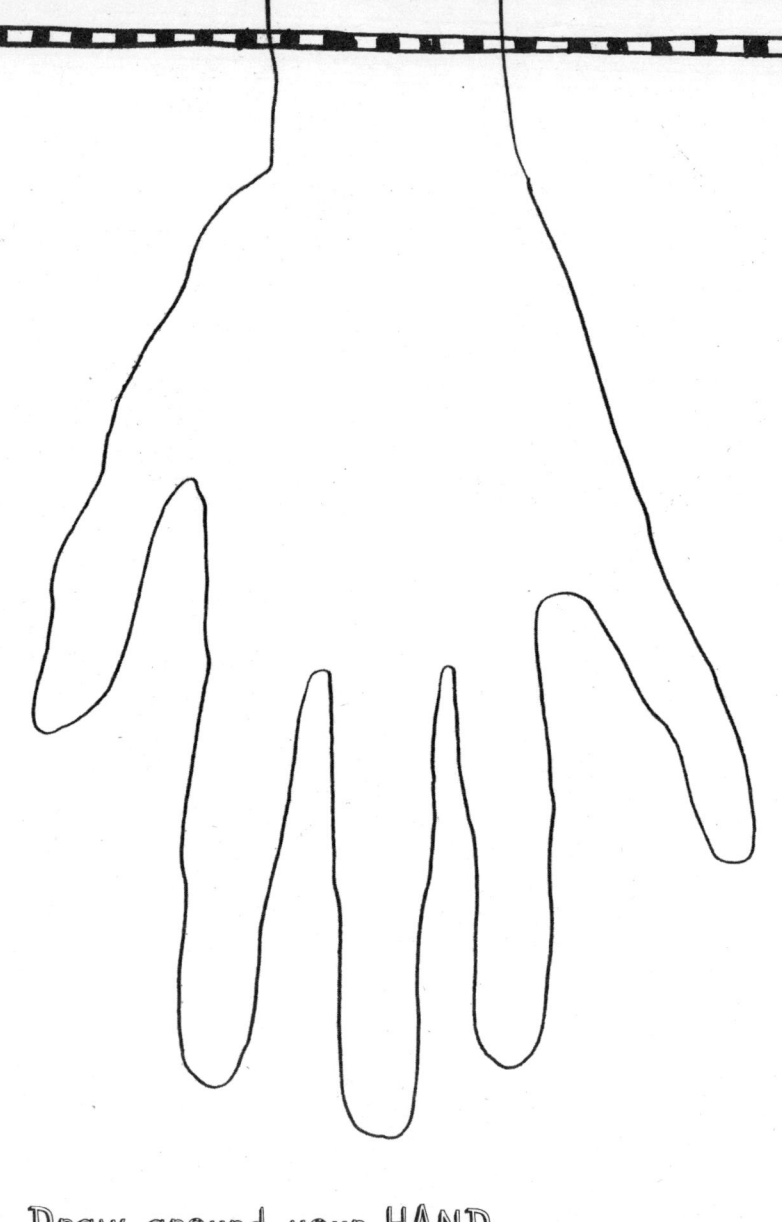

Draw around your HAND
and turn it into something ELSE.

Page to draw around your HAND

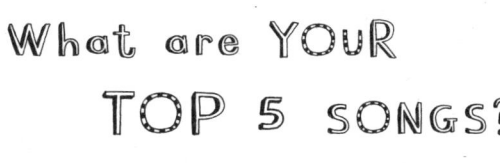

What are YOUR TOP 5 SONGS?

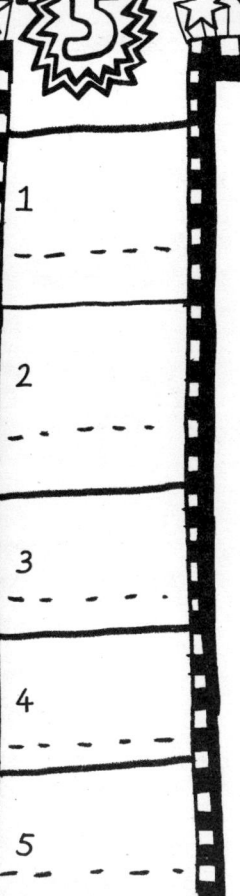

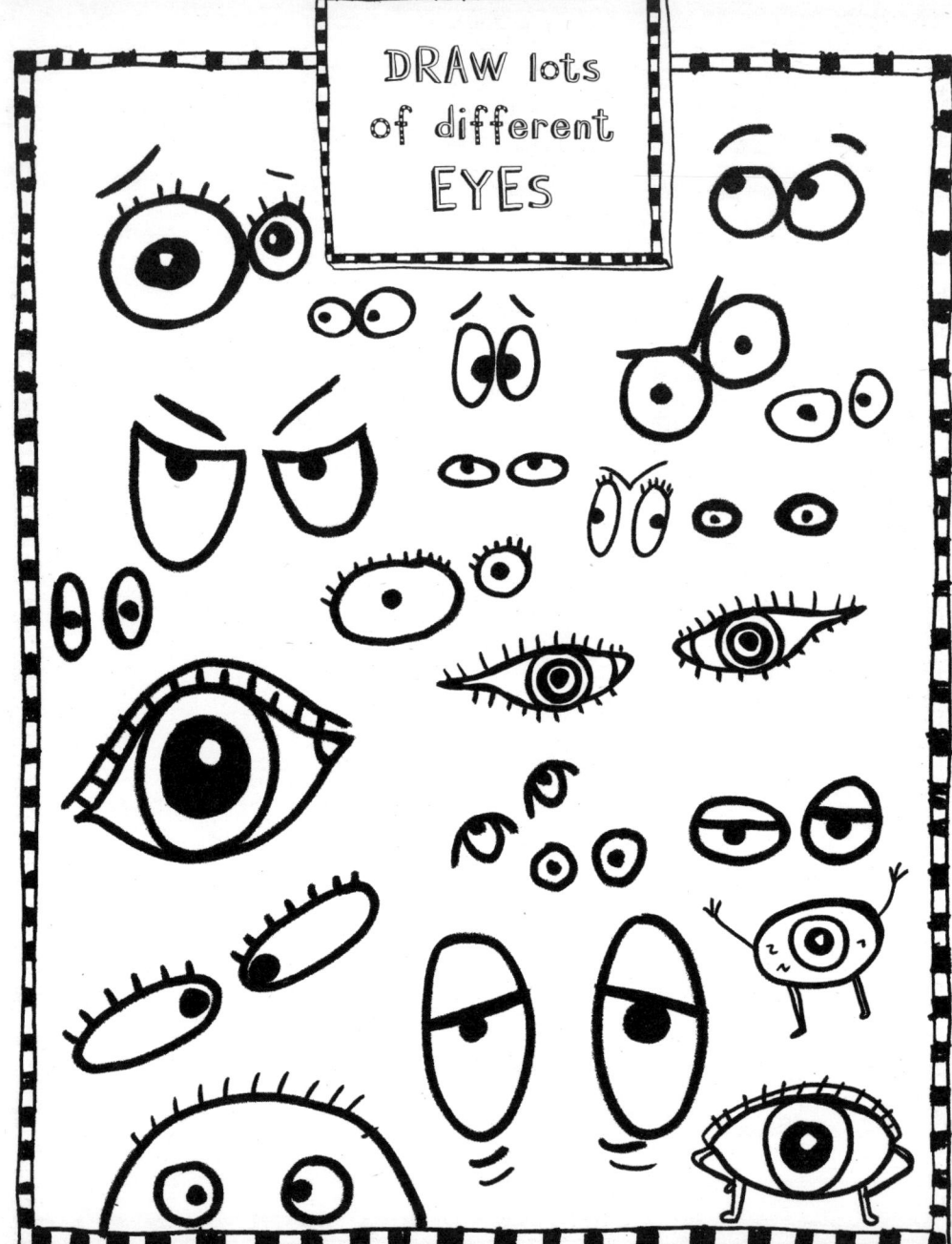

Eye eye

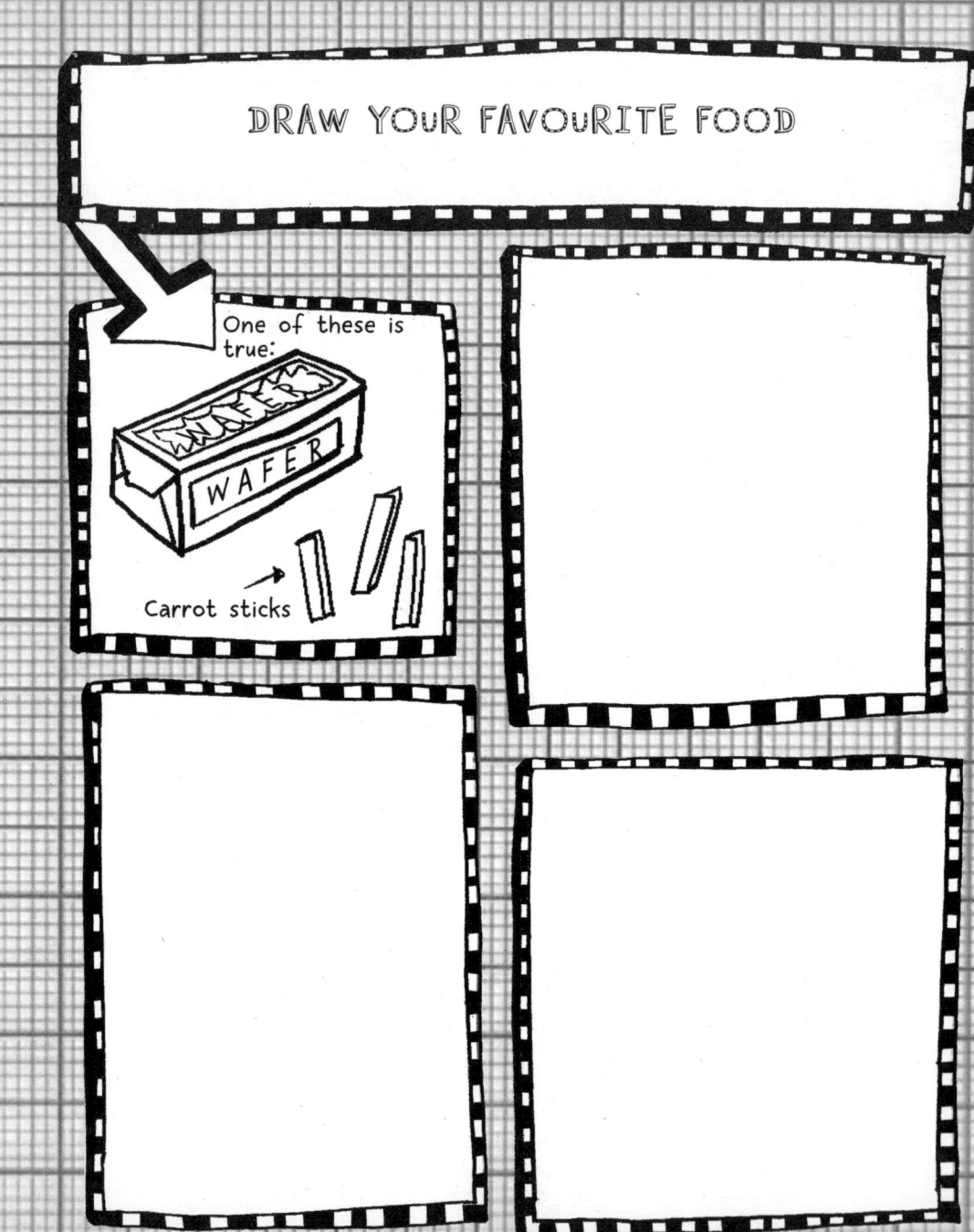

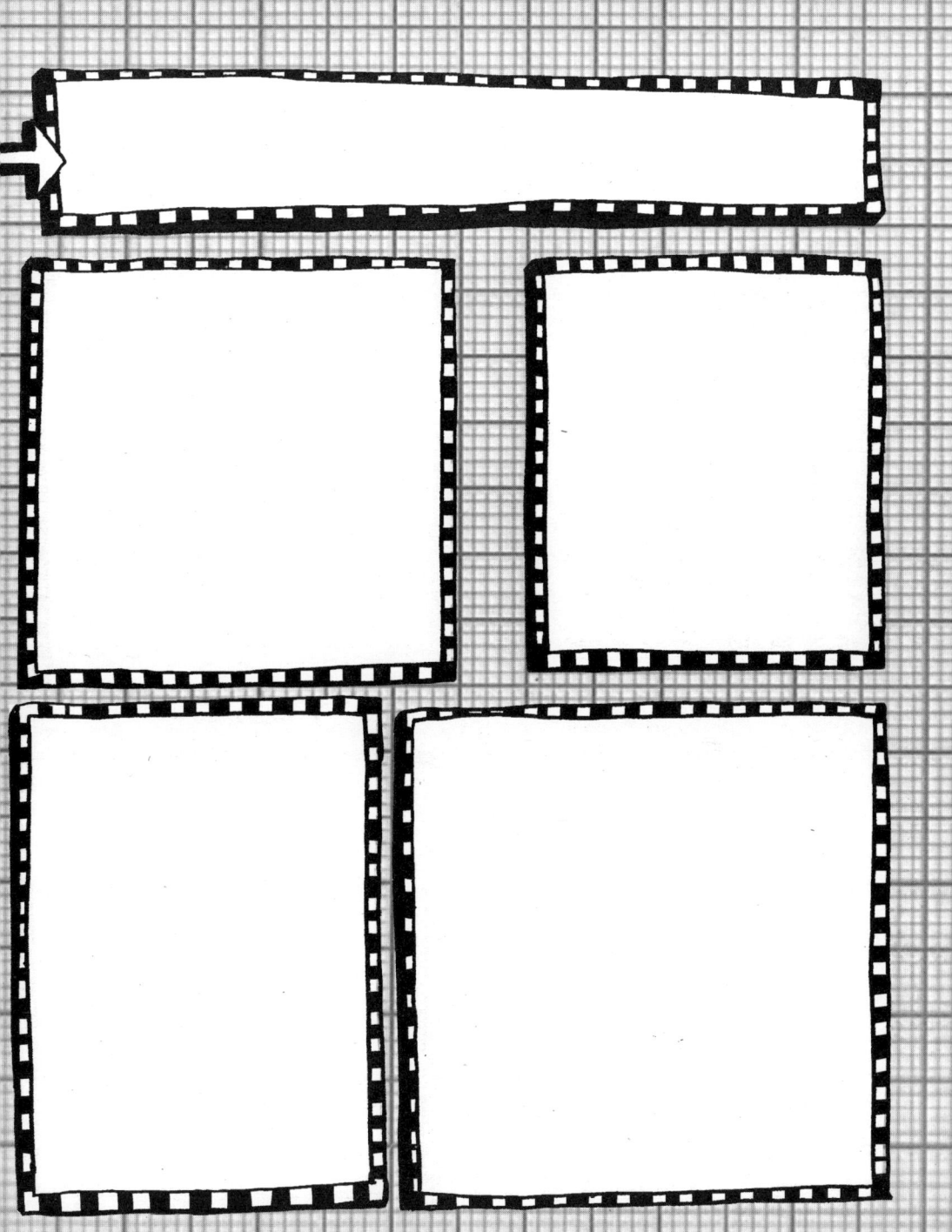

Scribble a Picture

Delia is surrounded by...

What is Delia standing on?

STICK photos of anything and EVERYTHING on these pages. (Do write WHEN, WHERE, WHO is in the photo. You WILL forget!)

Band practice didn't exactly go to plan. Who knew it would be THAT hard to play our instruments in the COLD and with gloves on?

Drinking hot chocolate to warm up has helped a LOT, but we still haven't done much practising. (None, to be exact.)

"After we've finished our hot chocolate shall we go back and have

another go?" I suggest to Norman, Leroy and Derek.

"Yes, we should," Leroy agrees.

"We need to write a new song as well," Derek reminds us.

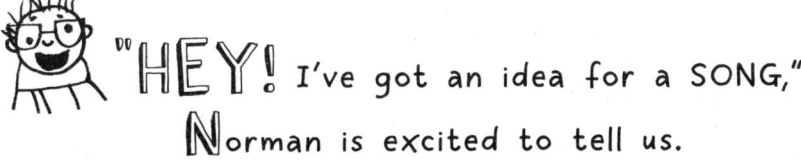"HEY! I've got an idea for a SONG," Norman is excited to tell us.

"GREAT! What's it about?" I ask.

"CHEESE — and how much I like it," Norman says.
(This is not a surprise as Norman is always talking about cheese.)

"Shall I sing it for you?" he adds.
Me and Derek say no, but Leroy says,
"LET'S hear it then."

Norman puts down his hot chocolate and stands in front of us and the TV. He's very STILL before he starts. And then...

Norman's cheese song is unexpectedly catchy.

 "What do you think?"
Norman wants to know.

"It's a cheese CLASSIC," I say.

 "I don't even like
cheese and I could sing this song," Leroy adds.

 "I've got CHEESE stuck in my head. Yes please
— to cheese," Derek tells Norman, who
seems happy.

"Do mice really like cheese?" I ask.

"They do — and they like chocolate too,"
Norman tells me.

(Mice have good taste.)

Norman asks us a RANDOM question.

"If you were a cheese, what cheese would you be?"

(This gets us thinking.)

Eventually I say ... "A cheese triangle!"

Leroy doesn't like cheese so he says,

"Cheese ... CAKE!"

"I'd be CHEDDAR – shall we go back to band practice?"

Derek suggests before Norman starts going off on one.

"How many times can you say 'cheese' in THIRTY SECONDS?"

We all take this as a CHALLENGE.

Derek has a stopwatch on his phone as we each have a go.

 Cheese cheese CHEESE cheese cheese cheese
Cheese CHEESE CHEESE cheese cheese cheeeeee

CHEESE CHEESE cheese cheese cheeeeee
Cheese cheese cheese cheese

 CHEESE CHEESE CHEESE CHEESE
Cheese cheese cheese cheese cheese cheeeeeese

Cheese cheese CHEESE cheese cheese cheese CHEESE
Cheese CHEESE CHEESE cheese cheese cheeeeee
Cheese cheese cheese cheese cheese

Norman is easily the winner, with Leroy a close second. This game takes a while and we should really get back to band practice.

 "I've warmed up now," Leroy says.

"Let's go then," Derek agrees.

It's important for **DOGZOMBIES** to keep practising all our songs if we want to be the best band EVER...

But then...

Derek's dad calls out.

(There's always tomorrow.)

SPACE FOR YOUR OWN STORY

DRAW PICTURES to GO with YOUR STORY

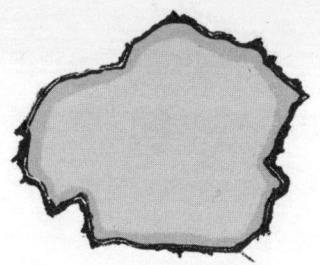

What has eaten
the page?

Rooster needs a SNACK
(or two, or three).

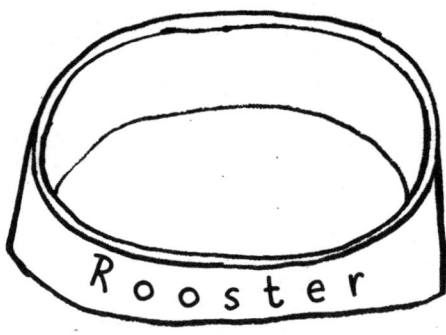

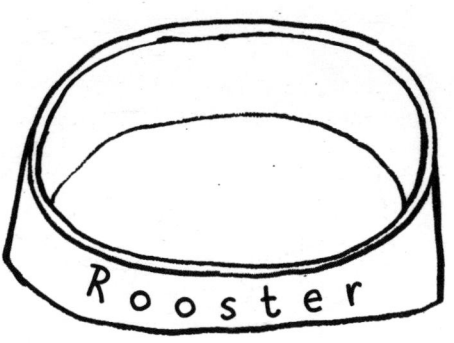

TuRN THESE NuMBERs INTO MONSTERs

1

2

3

4

5

HATS PLEASE

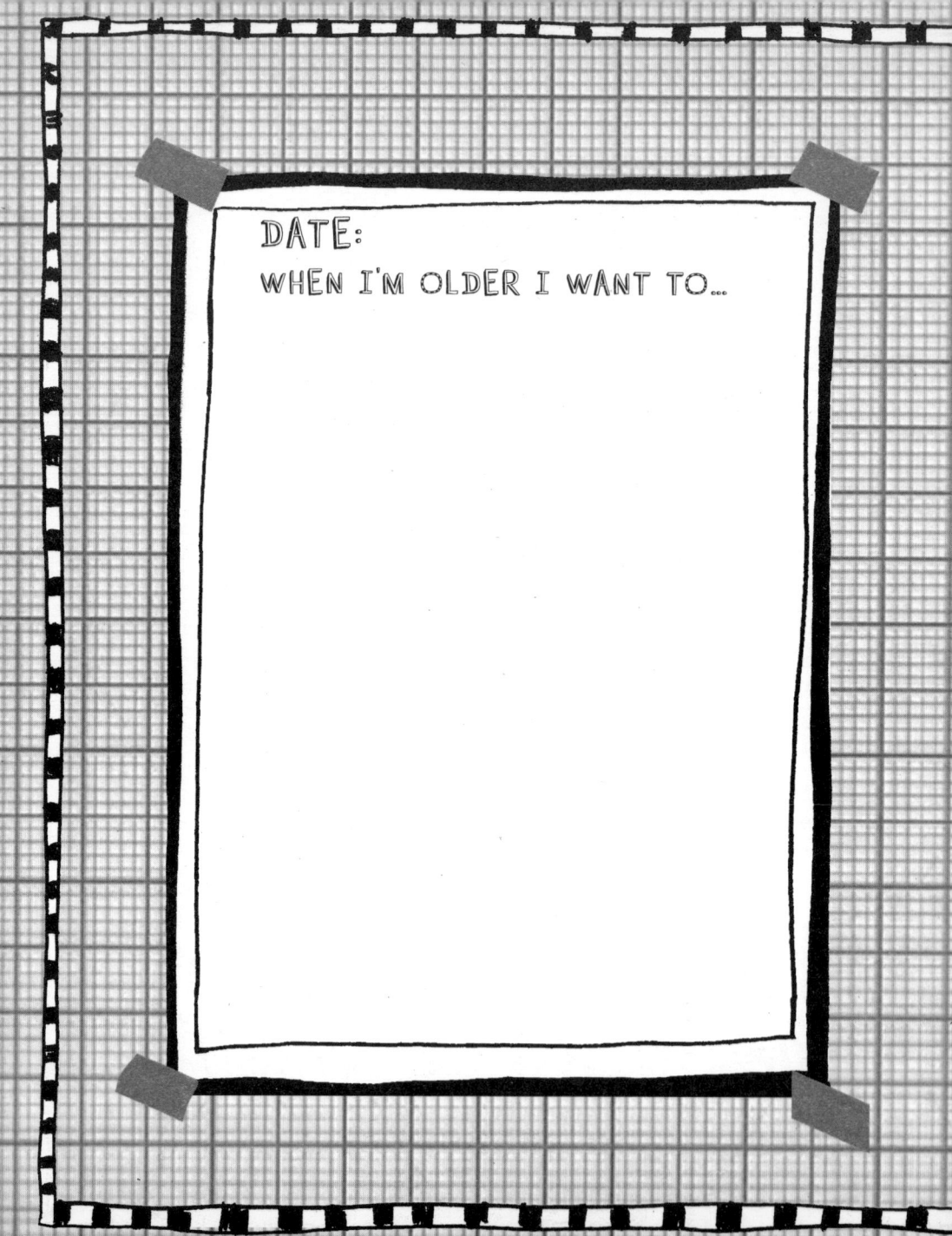

DATE:
WHEN I'M OLDER I WANT TO...

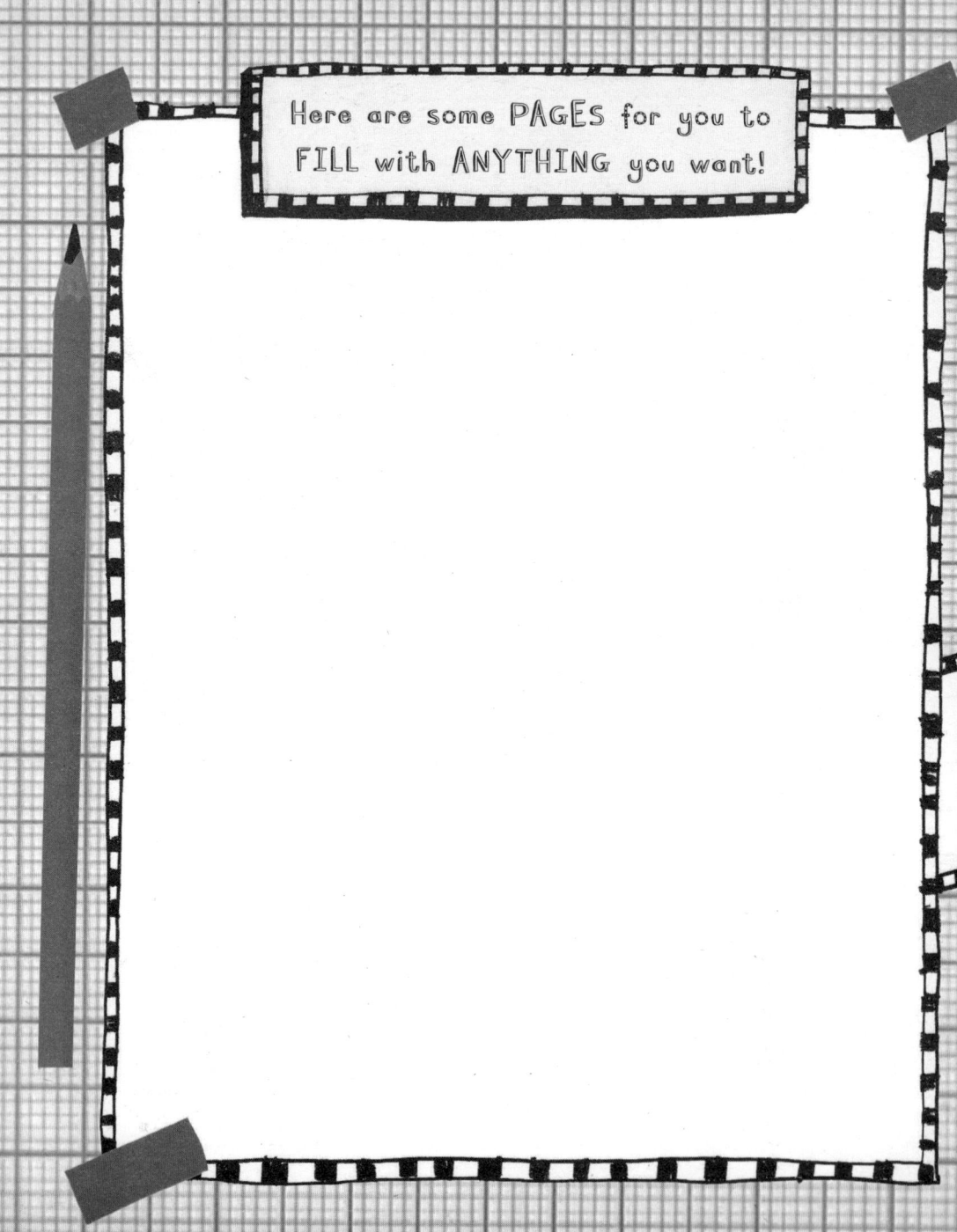

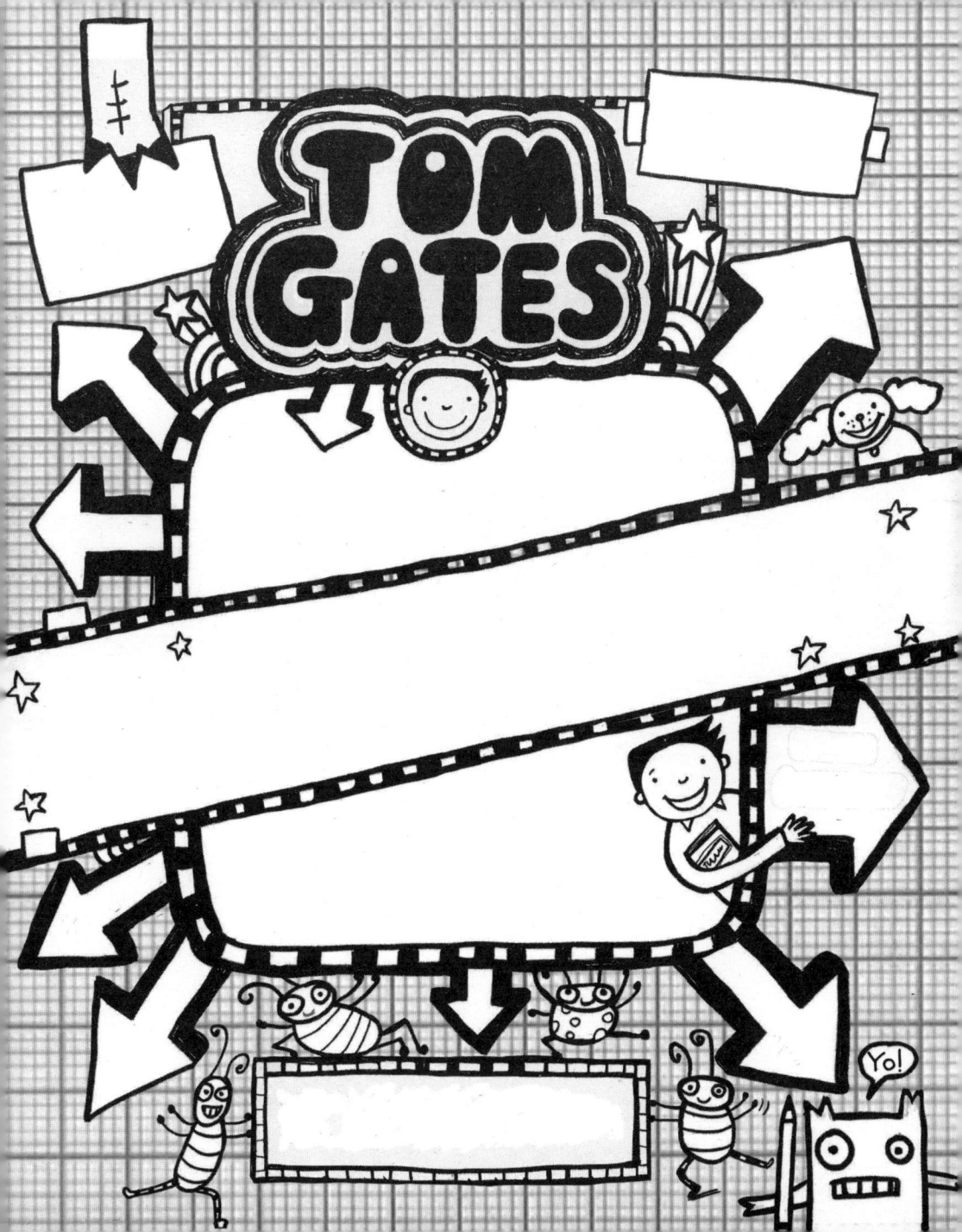

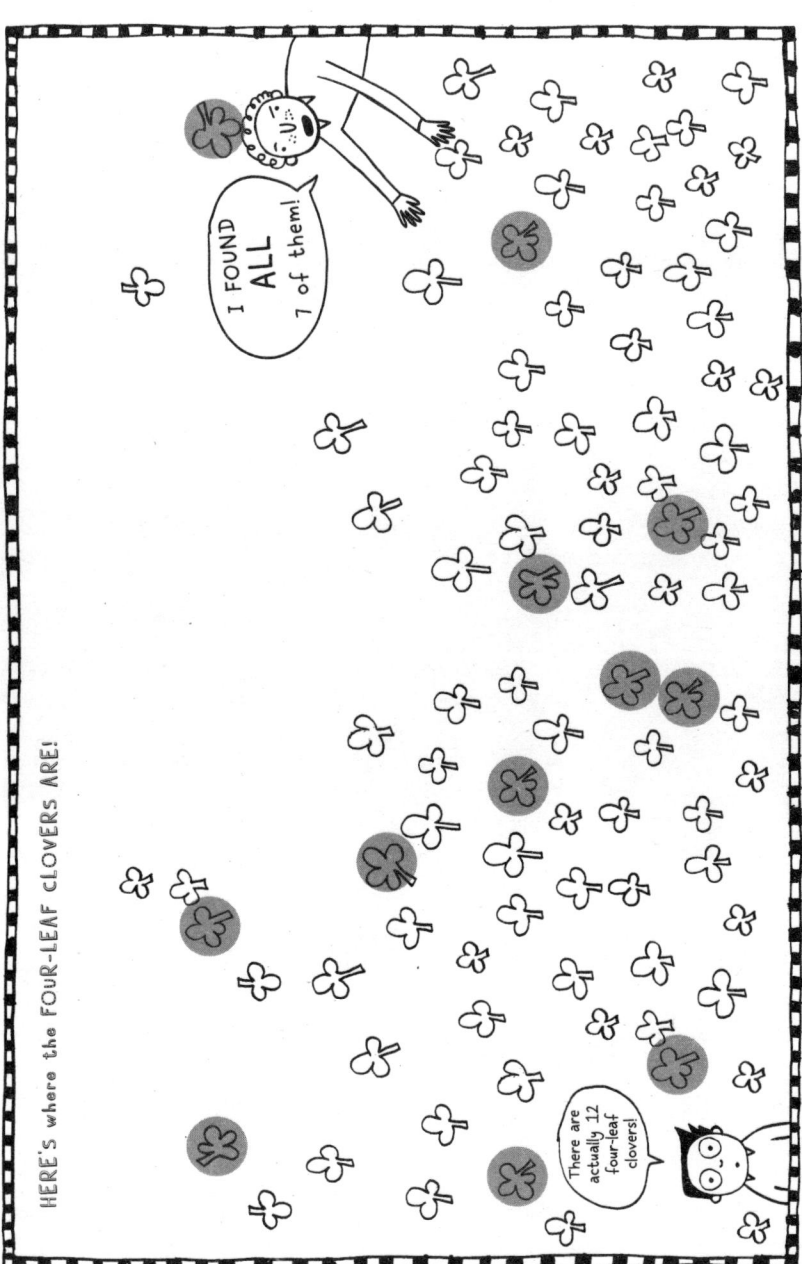

For more fun stuff...
visit thebrilliantworldoftomgates.com

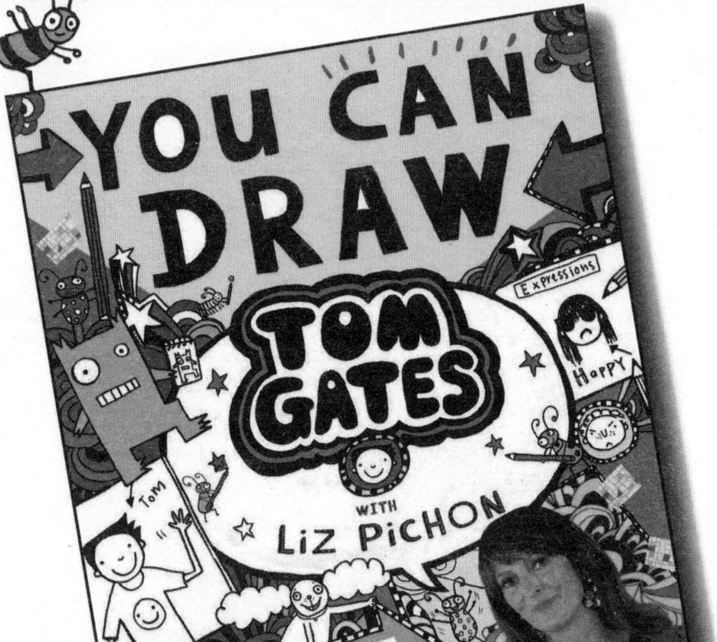

Learn to draw step-by-step people, places and objects from Tom's world.

The must-have art activity book for fans of Tom Gates.

From DOGZOMBIES to DUDE3, music is a HUGE part of the Tom Gates world. Learn how to play all your favourite songs from the series with REAL notation for:

- Guitar
- Piano
- Ukulele
- Recorder

And with notation for drums and tips and tricks for vocals!

Read all the Tom Gates books? Well, now you can read **SHOE WARS**, a standalone adventure story.

A Sunday Times Children's Book of the Year pick.

"Bursting with imagination and fabulous gadgets, **Shoe Wars** is full of Pichon's characteristic warmth, humour and quirky illustrations"
The Bookseller

"A tale oozing creativity and packed with pen and ink illustrations, exciting and expressive typography and visual jokes" *BookTrust*

Welcome to Shoe Town – and meet Ruby and Bear Foot. They are running out of time to rescue their inventor dad from his hideous boss, Wendy Wedge. She'll do ANYTHING to win the glitzy Golden Shoe Award and knows that entering flying shoes is her hot ticket to the trophy. Flying shoes that Ruby and Bear just happen to be hiding...

Liz Pichon is one of the UK's best-loved and bestselling creators of children's books. Her TOM GATES series has been translated into 45 languages, sold millions of copies worldwide, and has won the Roald Dahl Funny Prize, the Blue Peter Book Award for Best Story and the younger fiction category of the Waterstones Children's Book Prize. The TOM GATES books have inspired the nation's children to get creative, whether that's through reading, drawing, doodling, writing, making music or performing.

"I wanted to FILL the books with ALL the things I loved doing when I was a kid. It's just the best feeling ever to know children are enjoying reading the books, because I love making them. So thank you so much for choosing Tom Gates and keep reading and doodling!"

Visit Liz at www.lizpichon.com

(School photo of Liz being grumpy)